AND NOW WE ARE FOUR

AND NOW WE ARE FOUR

Pat Bilow

aven books
Division of Logos International
Plainfield, N.J. 07060

All Scripture references are taken from the King James Version unless otherwise noted TLB (The Living Bible) or RSV (Revised Standard Version).

AND NOW WE ARE FOUR
Copyright © 1980 by Logos International
All rights reserved
Printed in the United States of America
Library of Congress Catalog Number: 80-82577
International Standard Book Number: 0-88270-448-6
Logos International, Plainfield, New Jersey 07060

Dedication

To mom and dad, whose early love and care provided in my life a solidarity the Caseys of today so desperately seek.

Preface

The erosion of the traditional family unit is a fact of life in today's society. Consider these statistics cited in a recent communication distributed by United Way of America:

- The divorce rate has increased 113 percent.
- Fifteen percent of all families are now headed by women.
- More than one-third of all children under eighteen are not living with both natural parents.
- The number of children in foster care has increased by 37 percent.
- Sixteen percent of all couples are physically abusive.

Identity conflicts reign in these changing times, particularly for those children without suitable role models. Whether it be as a foster parent, weekend parent, Big Brother or Big Sister, concerned persons everywhere are needed to help temporarily homeless children survive the in-limbo state of foster care. Should this book pique your interest in this unnatural state of being, it will have served its purpose.

Contents

Preface
1 Tragedy Strikes   1
2 A New Door Opens   7
3 Interviews, Paperwork and Inspections!   17
4 Negative Responses From Family and Friends   27
5 Sweet Anticipation   35
6 And Now We Are Five   41
7 And One More Makes Six   47
8 Reassessing Those Priorities!   55
9 Adjusting to Special Problems   63
10 Family Ties That Bind   77
11 "Why, God?"   85
12 A Prompt Answer Plus Bonus!   95
13 Casey's New Home   109
14 Casey Rebels   119
15 "And I Feel the World Is Coming to an End"   133
16 A Negative Turns Into Positives   145
17 And the Lord Makes Lemonade!   153

AND NOW WE ARE FOUR

chapter one
Tragedy Strikes

The mood was quite relaxed. An almost festive air permeated the large office area as twenty of us prepared to devour an ethnic potluck luncheon fit for a king. Being relatively new in an accommodating, two-day-a-week position as a writer, I was told that once or twice a year each office employee contributed his favorite ethnic dish for one of those super deluxe luncheons that puts everyone to sleep around three.

I eyed the lasagna for a third time. My eyes said yes, but I heeded the feeling from my stomach that warned one more bite may set off an explosion.

It was good to relax and forget about the tension experienced during the last month. The subject turned to John Denver's upcoming concert in our community. I loved John Denver's music and his adept guitar playing. No matter that our seats were in the second from the last row. The kids and I weren't about to miss this concert for anything.

"Telephone call, Pat," someone called out to me in the midst of our John Denver conversation.

I picked up the nearest phone, wondering who

would be calling during lunch hour. It was my husband, Earl.

"Pat, come home right away." The urgency in his voice spelled tragedy.

"What is it, Earl? Tell me—what's happened?"

"No, Pat, I can't. Just come home and look at the house," he pleaded.

I quickly excused myself, cleared off my office desk, and was on my way.

It had to be Casey. Dear God, did he have an accident? Had he, as a runaway, fallen into the wrong hands and been assaulted? Oh, Lord, what if he's dead? Oh, no, that must be it. Earl told me to look at the house. He wants me to remember how many years just the four of us lived in that house and how precious a gift from God our family was.

I thought and prayed all the way home. Casey—dear, sweet, fourteen-year-old Casey. Why couldn't he accept the love and care we offered him? Why did he keep running away? Was it his friendship with Craig?

When Casey came into our home as a foster child eight months before, what a smooth transition he made. Casey blossomed in a family environment—especially after living in an institution for three years. Casey and our oldest son Mark—what a combination! Two fourteen-year-old boys in the same family. Never was there a dull moment—nor an unused phone. How two gangly young teenagers, good-looking as they

TRAGEDY STRIKES

were, could attract so many girls was beyond me. Eleven-year-old Matt couldn't for the life of him understand such an interest in the opposite sex.

What had happened? When did that fine delicate balance that keeps a family in sync begin to slip? If one member in the body of Christ suffers, all members suffer, Paul taught in his first letter to the Corinthians. How true that is! The turmoil Casey experienced during the recent weeks affected each member of our family—Earl, myself, Mark, and Matt.

Driving around the final corner of the seemingly endless journey home, I spotted two police cars parked by our curb. Matt walked out through the back door, sobbing uncontrollably.

"Matt, honey, what's wrong?" I asked him shakily.

"It's terrible, mom," he replied between heaving sobs. "Just go in and see."

My knees started to buckle, but somehow I made it through the back door into the kitchen. My eyes gazed on an unbelievable sight. The kitchen was in shambles. The floor and dining room carpet were littered with soap powders, canned food contents, milk, cat food, and dog food. A drawer had been emptied on the floor. Raw eggs peppered the cupboard doors and paneled walls. The flour canisters looked like targets for an old-fashioned egg-throwing contest. Raw eggs lay on the counter top a quarter of an inch thick.

How many of the six dozen eggs I had just

bought for Easter were used? I gasped when I opened the refrigerator door to check. The inside was sprayed with red paint. Not one egg was left. The stove and dishwasher, too, had been spray painted. Even the coffee inside the coffeepot wasn't spared from the ever-present ugly paint.

Earl led me by the arm into the living room. Two sympathetic police officers looked on as I broke into tears. The living room was even worse. The big pot of bean soup Earl had made the night before was strewn all over the carpet, as were other food items, broken lamps, and the daily mail torn to shreds. A big red cross was sprayed on the mirror of the guest closet door, another target for eggs. An obscenity sprayed on the upholstered chair that matched the davenport leaped out like a glaring neon sign. The word, "Goodbye," adorned one papered wall in the dining room. Every few minutes brought a new devastation to our eyes.

"Is this it?" I tearfully asked one of the officers.

He shook his head in sympathy. "I'm sorry. The upstairs and your recreation room in the basement are just as bad. Better sit for a while before you tackle the rest." It was the worst vandalism destruction he and his partner had ever seen, he added.

The officer told me how all the books from the bookshelves downstairs were thrown on the carpeted floor and the furniture overturned on top of them. The conglomeration was then doused with bleach, kerosene, and lighter fluid. Had Matt not interrupted Casey and his friend, Craig, when he came home from school for lunch, would a match next have been lit?

I glanced around the living room. Every article adorning the walls was devastated in one way or another—save one. Hanging above the obscenity-inscribed chair was the gold cross and two plaques Earl had put up several years ago. "In quietness and in confidence shall be your strength" (Isa. 30:15) read one. The other: "The will of God will never lead you where the grace of God cannot keep you." Behind the tangible results of hatred and defiance seen in every room of the house was an intangible plea that cried, "Please help me!" The untouched cross and verses stood out as if to answer, "Yes, there is a way. Come and follow me."

> When you go through deep waters and great trouble, I will be with you. When you go through the rivers of difficulty, you will not drown! When you walk through the fire of oppression, you will not be burned up—the flames will not consume you. (Isa. 43:2, TLB)

chapter two
A New Door Opens

As I lay in the dark motel room late at night, unable to sleep, question after question remained unanswered. Where were Casey and Craig now? Did they have food? Where were they sleeping? Would they return to the house? Why had God allowed this to happen? I knew that "all things work together for good to them that love God, to them who are the called according to his purpose" (Rom. 8:28). And I also knew the Lord in His inevitable perfect way had prepared us for this horrible tragedy.

In the quiet solitude of the night, my mind relived the past five years that had brought us to this point. Praise Him for His direction in our lives. He knew my full-time job was taking me further away from our family. So He channeled our interest to my grandmother's eighty-acre farm.

When I was very small, grandma rented the farm to accept my parents' offer to live with us in the city. Tenants occupied the farm for many years until a fire one day destroyed the house and several outbuildings. The house was never rebuilt.

Ten years after the fire, Earl and I took the boys

to the farm to spend a weekend in our camper in the overgrown weeds which once had been a well-manicured lawn. We set up camp, nestled in the shadow of the big old barn. Constructed in the late 1800s, the barn had remained untouched by the fire.

That weekend proved to be a turning point in our lives. The enthusiasm to convert the property to a weekend retreat spread quickly through each of us. In time our investment grew to a large mobile home complete with a big wooden porch/deck Earl and the boys constructed. It only seemed natural to pass on the joy and fun we found at the farm. What better way to do so than to invite temporarily homeless boys for weekends of running off excess energy and frustrations?

Many people have asked how this idea came about. I honestly don't know. But I believe it was at the hand of the Lord. We knew no one who took children for weekends. We had no friends who were into foster care. There were no public service announcements heard on radio or television nor literature read. I recall just phoning a nearby children's home one day to get more information about "weekend" kids. After a family discussion on the subject the next day, I spent my lunch hour visiting the home and completing an application for us to become "weekend" parents.

Our farm weekends with our young guests gave us an exposure to a world of which I was only faintly aware. In many of the boys bottled-up feelings of insecurity and frustration were tragically enacted. One guest, ten-year-old Tommy, seethed with anger when he failed to win a race on Matt's bicycle. So he rammed the bike against the barn. Mark and Matt hesitated from then on to share any of their belongings. Another boy, Steve, enjoyed Mark's coin collection—so much so that he ripped off part of it. Eight-year-old Tim rejected friendly gestures made by our boys, preferring rather to cling (like glue!) to Earl and myself. He desperately sought parental love and acceptance.

The physical pain and emotional hurt to which so many had been subjected expressed itself through undesirable behavior patterns like bed-wetting, inflicting physical pain on others, moodiness, and general unhappiness.

Paul writes in his letter to the Romans that "tribulation worketh patience" (Rom. 5:3). I firmly believe the Lord used our weekends with homeless children to prepare our family to learn patience for the new venture He had in store for us. He exposed to us a new wrinkle in society that man carelessly created through yet another of his mistakes—the insecure world of misplaced children. Children who live in an in-limbo state for an undetermined period of time. Children who know far too many insecurities, doubts, and fears. Children who come from broken families and near-poverty conditions. Children who do not understand why.

My friend Shirley Stretchbery is the supervisor of the foster homes department of a midwest county children's home which currently has 350 children placed in 260 foster homes. She says, "Separating a child from his parents is always a traumatic experience for that child. He feels grief in addition to guilt. The child actually goes through a mourning process which is often repeated after he leaves a foster home. The foster parents have to be trained to give a lot of themselves to the child, often not receiving anything back."

This, perhaps, explains the constantly changing population of foster parents. Often, emotional ties develop between the foster child and foster family. Many foster families cannot withstand the pain of breaking these ties when the foster child is eventually returned to his real parents. Fostering becomes an emotional drain.

It was four years ago that God initiated for us the transition from being weekend parents to becoming foster parents.

Down the one-lane country road at the farm, six small figures on bicycles, followed by two playful dogs, slowly appeared crossing the bridge. One lone figure, peddling for all she was worth, brought up the rear.

"Hey, wait for me, you guys," she cried. "I can't go that fast!"

A NEW DOOR OPENS

The bicycle brigade (Mark and Matt—then twelve and nine—and three neighboring farm boys) wheeled their bikes to the side of the road and waited.

Little did I realize how God would use this little peddling straggler to turn our family's lives around. This particular weekend we expected to have nine-year-old Jimmy. But Sister Marie from the children's home had called earlier in the week with a change in plans.

"Mrs. Bilow, we have a small problem," she told me over the phone. "Jimmy's caseworker has scheduled a visit with his mother."

"Oh, I understand," I said, somewhat disappointed. "May we have someone else?"

"I know you have requested only boys," she went on. "But how about taking a little girl for a change?"

Well, why not? The female species in our household had been outnumbered three to one (and more at times) for fifteen years. Funny that I never thought much about it, but rarely did little girls visit our home. Our sons' friends, up to this point, were always male. A little girl, even for just a weekend, would be a delight.

And now, here she was. Living up to—no, exceeding—our expectations.

"Hi, Jenny," I greeted her after returning home from work. Shyly and with her head ever so slightly bowed, Jenny returned the greeting.

She was so small. It looked as though the chair would swallow her up. Her short legs stuck straight out. And her feet, resting against each other in pigeon-toed fashion, were clad in well-worn tennis shoes. Dressed in bib overalls and wearing her long dark hair in braids, seven-year-old, brown-eyed Jenny looked every bit a tomboy—half-pint sized.

Earl and the boys soon had the car packed, ready to leave for the farm. I locked the back door to the house while Jenny waited. As we walked toward the car, Jenny shyly slipped her little hand in mine.

Once at the farm, Jenny's shyness gave way to comfort and assurance. Apprehensions faded as she performed routine tasks with me, like stirring frosting for our freshly baked cupcakes.

"I love to frost cupcakes," she said as a big drop of chocolate icing fell from her knife to the floor.

"I think you like to sample it, too, don't you Jenny?" I teased, noting her frosting-speckled mouth. Jenny laughed as she wiped her mouth with her hand.

"Hey, you know what?" she asked.

"Jenny, you don't know what to call me, do you?" I smiled. Jenny looked embarrassed as she lowered her head. "How about my giving you a choice, OK? Would you rather call me Mrs. Bilow or Aunt Pat?"

"I'd like to call you Aunt Pat," she grinned, quickly regaining her composure.

"Then Aunt Pat it is," I said leaning down to hug her. "Now what did you want to tell me?"

"I'm afraid to say it."

"Do you think I'll laugh?"

"No."

"Then, why won't you tell me, Jenny?"

"I don't know."

"Oh, go ahead," I coaxed as I tickled her ribs.

Jenny laughed and said, "OK, but promise not to tell."

"I won't breathe a word."

"I really like you and your daddy," she said softly. "And Mark and Matt, too."

"Earl is my husband, and that's a very nice compliment, Jenny," I smiled. "I like us too." We both laughed.

I knew that Jenny was the little girl I had always wanted. A selfish motive, but nevertheless a true one.

Then, one dreary, drizzling Sunday evening about a month after we met Jenny, Mark surprisingly enough brought up the subject of foster care. Earl had returned Jenny only several hours earlier to the children's home (which, I might add, is a far cry from the negative connotation that an institution usually implies) after a weekend visit.

"Jenny said she wants to live in a foster home like two of her sisters," Mark said as his eyes sparkled enthusiastically. "And she wants to live with us. How about it, mom and dad?"

"Yuk!" Matt exclaimed, dropping his fork with a loud clang on the plate. "You're in love with her, Mark. I don't want to live with *any* girls."

"What about mom?" Mark countered. "She's a girl."

"Mom's different."

"Thanks, Matt," I offered.

Earl bemusedly listened to the banter at the dinner table until it slipped from the discussion level into a heated disagreement. Nine-year-old Matt clearly didn't want any female invading his private domain. Girls delighted only in telling secrets not meant to be shared, showing off in front of teachers, and jumping rope for lack of anything better to do. Who needed them?

On the other hand, Cupid's arrow had winged its way directly to twelve-year-old Mark. It landed dead center. Mark was smitten—with love for Jenny.

The air was getting hot and heavy.

"That's enough!" Earl boomed as he slammed his hand on the table for order. "No more arguing, you two. We've got to do some serious thinking.

"Matt, you would have to give up your bedroom. Mark, do you want to share yours? Think of the extra work involved and the adjustments each of us must be willing to make to bring Jenny into the family. She needs a lot of love, discipline, and guidance. Can we give these things to her? Are we willing to give them to her?"

A NEW DOOR OPENS

It was not a decision to approach lightly. Adding a new member—especially one with an entirely different background—to any family circle is not easy. Each of us would have to vote affirmatively. Otherwise, it wouldn't work.

I actually wanted to satisfy a very selfish need—the need for my own little girl. Why, then, didn't I become pregnant? First, I could not be guaranteed a girl. Second, I truly enjoyed older children more than babies. And, third, the world already is overpopulated. Why not take an existing child who has no parents, even if temporarily, rather than add one of my own? I entered foster care possessively, hoping that that child would one day be mine. Since that time, I have learned the true meaning of foster care—to maintain and strengthen the foster child's own home.

We prayed about our decision and concentrated on how Jenny's entrance into the family would affect each of us. Would I be able to handle full-time employment with this added responsibility? Was I willing to give up some of my own time to prepare extra food, wash and fold more clothes, and clean up after one more person? Deep in my heart, the answer was yes to every question I asked myself.

Seven days later, I called Mrs. Taylor, Jenny's caseworker. We had reached a decision. Earl, Mark, and Matt had also answered yes to their questions. Our family would open a new door to explore a world very foreign to our own. A world filled with much exhilaration and, most certainly, many heartbreaks. A gray world of insecure children . . . guilt-ridden parents . . . inundated caseworkers. We were about to enter the intriguing world of the foster child.

> Ask, and it shall be given you; seek, and ye shall find; knock, and it shall be opened unto you. (Matt. 7:7; Luke 11:9)

chapter three
Interviews, Paperwork and Inspections!

"Mom, we finished cleaning our room," Matt shouted down the clothes chute from the bathroom. The chute also substituted for an intercom, conveniently relaying messages from one floor to the next.

I opened the chute door in the breakfast nook. "I'll be up in a second, Matt, as soon as the kitchen is finished."

In the next room, Raisin, our black lab, playfully attacked the vacuum cleaner while Earl tried to sweep the dining room carpet.

I glanced at the clock. 7:10 P.M. Where did the time go? Mrs. Taylor was scheduled to arrive in twenty minutes to conduct a home study for our foster care license. What was that old game show on TV? "Beat the Clock"—that was it. Here we were, I mused, playing our own little game of "Beat the Clock."

Well, at least the kitchen is cleaned, I thought to myself as I wiped my hand on a towel. Bzzz. Oh, great, the telephone. But there wasn't time for any interruptions. I picked up the receiver.

"How do you do, Mrs. Billow?"

"It's Bilow. One *l*."

"Oh, forgive me, Mrs. Bi-low. May I ask, do you own your residence on Maxwell?" A salesman. Why do they always call at the wrong time?

The doorbell sang through our mundane conversation. I quickly cut off the caller. Ready or not, this was it. I could hear Mrs. Taylor introduce herself to Earl and the boys. Drawing in a deep breath and saying a short prayer, I walked confidently into the living room. Mark and Matt held back Raisin while Earl took Mrs. Taylor's coat.

She was much younger than I expected. It seemed odd this thin young woman dressed in a tailored three-piece pantsuit and platform shoes would inspect each room of our house and evaluate every member of the family. What did I expect? A towering matron of authority who would pass judgment upon us?

Sandy, a friendly person who suggested we initiate our relationship on a first-name basis, efficiently pulled out what seemed like reams of forms. The questions came slowly at first, then picked up momentum as they increased in depth.

How do you discipline your children? Why do you want to be a foster parent? What is your annual income? How do you spend your money? Tell me a little about your childhood. How did your parents discipline you? Were you happy? What do you hope to derive from foster care?

The "interrogation," as Earl later called it,

continued for over an hour.

"We do go into a lot of detail," Sandy apologized. "But this is for the protection of the children."

"Of course. We understand," Earl replied.

We next led Sandy through each room of our home. As we approached the boys' bedrooms, I said another little prayer. Not that I didn't have faith in my sons, you understand! But this time I was pleasantly surprised. Even their growing beer can collections were neatly stacked, conveniently out of the way. Thank you, Lord, I thought to myself. The ability is there. They just need more motivation every now and then!

The home study completed, it was our turn to ask the questions.

"Sandy, can you give some background on Jenny?" I asked.

"Jenny's case is one of neglect," Sandy explained. "She has four sisters, all of whom have been in institutional or foster care for the past two years. Jenny's parents are now divorced. Her father drinks and was unable to provide any financial stability for the family. Her mother had her first child when still a teenager and subsequently has had ten or twelve pregnancies."

I almost couldn't believe what I was hearing. Jenny came from an entirely different world, so completely foreign to ours. Now, hopefully, God would entrust her care to our family. What a privilege it would be to nurture her in the word of Christ!

Jenny's mother presently was incapable of caring, at least temporarily, for her five girls, Sandy added. The care of her children plus several miscarriages and stillborn births had left her physically and mentally exhausted. The family had lived in an old house infested with mice and rats. Clothes lined the bedroom floors. There was no money to buy dressers for storage.

"We have had temporary custody of Jenny and her sisters for two years now," Sandy explained. "That means the girls are temporarily in our custody, and the parents hold rights to visit their children. If Jenny's parents voluntarily signed a permanent surrender or the courts awarded the county permanent custody (involuntary surrender), Jenny would be eligible for adoption."

"How likely is that to happen?" I asked.

"Chances are very slim," Sandy answered. "Very rarely does this occur. The courts heavily lean toward keeping families together."

Sandy told us Jenny had been very undisciplined when she came into the care of the children's home. While much had been accomplished there, she still needed to learn more about exercising self-discipline. Our work clearly was cut out for us. (She also stressed the importance of confidentiality in each foster care case. Consequently, names of foster children have been changed in this book to assure anonymity.)

"You won't get rich in this business," Sandy

INTERVIEWS, PAPERWORK AND INSPECTIONS!

laughed. "We pay $2.50 a day for children who are Jenny's age. The rate increases for teenagers and mentally or physically handicapped children."

(Since that time we have received a twenty-five cents per day raise. We, however, fostered children through a neighboring county in Ohio which pays lesser rates than our own. During 1976, the county in which we lived paid:

Age	Daily rate	Monthly clothing allowance
Birth-3	$2.60	$ 5
4-6	$2.85	$ 8
7-12	$3.00	$12
Teenagers	$3.50	$20

For mentally or physically handicapped children, the rate was $4.00 per day.

Columnist Sylvia Porter once devoted a column to foster care needs. In it she stated, "There is a real money incentive to keep a child in foster care." She reported during 1976 an average of $260 per month was paid per foster child. We, in fact, realized $75 per each thirty day month for Jenny's foster care. My sister and brother-in-law, who live in the state of Washington, earned approximately $100 per month per child during the same period. While Ms. Porter's figure seems high for that year, unfortunately some people are foster parents for the money they receive. Says one foster parent of a sixteen-year-old girl, "It can become almost a business. It depends on your economic station in life. For low-income families, one or two foster children can make a sizable difference in their income.")

As I listened to Sandy, I couldn't help but become mesmerized by this foreign way of life in which so many displaced children were forced to live.

"Sandy, how do children come into foster care?" I asked.

"Foster care is the result of any kind of trauma that upsets a family," she answered. "It could be a single mother who cannot cope any longer with the children, a father who has deserted the family, physical or emotional illness, child abuse, or substandard housing. But no matter the cause, it's a traumatic experience for a child to go through."

I began to realize the scope of God's special call for our family. I knew He would instill each of us with the necessary strength to provide the special care needed by each foster child entrusted to our care. Psalm 68:35 promised me that. ("The God of Israel gives strength and mighty power to his people," TLB.) But as we talked with Sandy, the responsibility we were about to undertake overwhelmed me. It's a good thing the Lord reveals His plan one step at a time. If I could have gazed into the future, I'm sure I would have bowed out—right then and there.

"I see no problem with your application to

become foster parents," Sandy told us. "But a few details still remain before we can submit everything to the state. We'll need six character reference letters from business associates and friends. Also, a statement of condition on the health of each of you from your medical doctor. Oh, and I almost forgot. We also need a fire inspection report from your local fire department. For those people living in rural areas, we order a well water test. But that, of course, won't be necessary in your case. Once we have all the necessary paper work, we'll send the whole ball of wax to the state."

(I later learned not all states require as much detail as ours to obtain a foster care license. Recently, I had an opportunity to talk with a caseworker for a southeastern county in the state of Washington. "We require only an approved home study, well water inspection in rural areas, three reference letters, and a TB test for each member of the family," she said. "Actually, it's very simple to get a foster care license here. Maybe too simple.")

"How long will it take the state to return our license?" Earl asked Sandy.

"Don't expect it for at least four or six weeks," she replied.

"Mom, do you think Jenny will be here by Christmas?" Mark wondered.

"I don't know, honey," I said doubtfully.

"Let's say there's a strong probability," Sandy added, "if—and that's a big if—we can get all the forms in within the next two weeks. I'll certainly try to do my part on time."

"What a Christmas gift—if we could have Jenny, eh, Mark?" Earl said. Mark shrugged his shoulders, trying hard to look indifferent in front of Sandy.

"One more question, Sandy," I said, "before you go. What about religious training for foster children?"

"We encourage foster parents to provide the opportunity for spiritual development through an appropriate religious affiliation which does not conflict with the religious beliefs of the child's parents," Sandy answered. "Jenny, however, has received some religious training from the children's home."

"Suffer little children, and forbid them not" (Matt. 19:14). These beautiful words of Christ popped into my mind from childhood memory work. Jenny had learned to love the Lord. But how many children like her never experience Christ's love for them because of inexposure to His Word?

Sandy packed her completed forms into an already full briefcase. As she left our house, I watched her trek to an old station wagon through newly fallen snow. She was a compassionate person. I thought how difficult it must be for her to remain detached from some of her cases.

I turned off the porch light after Sandy pulled

away. All the mental tension and physical activity of the past several days spread through me as I collapsed on the davenport. My eyelids closed heavily. All of a sudden, every bone in my body ached. But I felt so good inside.
"If you pour yourself out for the hungry and satisfy the desire of the afflicted, then shall your light rise in the darkness and your gloom be as the noonday." (Isa. 58:10, RSV)

chapter four
Negative Responses From Family and Friends

The word spread quickly. At work, in church, throughout the neighborhood, and even at the farm. The Bilows are taking in that cute, little dark-haired girl they call "Jenny." You know, the one who spends so many weekends with them.

Where are her parents? Don't they want her? Have you ever seen her little sister? Ann—that's her name. Sometimes she comes with Jenny for the weekends . . . Poor girls. I've heard they've lived at the children's home for two years now . . . You say there's five of them altogether? Three at the children's home and two in foster homes? Isn't that a shame . . . Well, I don't know. It's nice they're taking her in. But I don't think I'd want to tackle a problem like that. Pat calls her "free-spirited." She's unruly, if you ask me . . . She'll need a lot of discipline and attention. Is that really fair to their boys? It's going to be hard on them . . . No, foster care is not for me. It's a drain physically and mentally . . . And who needs that? Besides, look how hard it would be when the child leaves . . . No, I don't think so. I've got enough to handle with my own family.

Feedback resounded even from the outer rims of friendship. Some people felt we were performing a good deed "above and beyond the call of duty." Others questioned the effect fostering would have on our boys. Still others remained silent—some preferring to take a laissez-faire approach, while others seriously questioned our motives.

I later discovered we were fortunate. None of us had been exposed to such crude remarks as, "I don't see how you can take in those county kids—I couldn't" or, "Of course, you get paid for it," like some foster parents hear. Take, for example, thirty-five-year-old Mr. B. He grew up in a total of nine or ten foster homes. He doesn't remember the exact number; it was easy to lose count after a while. Because of his own experiences, Mr. B. knew he could help foster children. So he and his wife became licensed foster parents.

I first met Mr. and Mrs. B. two years ago when I interviewed them for an article I was writing. Some of his childhood experiences in foster care were chilling, to say the least.

When Mr. B. proudly told a few of his eighteen brothers and sisters about his new status as a foster parent, he says, "They all thought I was insane. And they weren't afraid to tell me so either."

Like Mr. B., Donna Harbison, a devout Christian whom I came to know through my sister, grew up in foster care in the Pacific Northwest. In addition to raising their own five, Donna and her husband, Don, have five foster children. ("My husband has accepted me for what I am," Donna told me recently. "If a kid literally knocks at my door asking for a place to live—and that has happened—Don knows I'm going to let him in. This is my whole life.")

Donna still hears negative comments about her large family. "People don't understand what it's like to be a foster child," she told me one morning as we sat around my sister's kitchen table. "I know what some of these kids are going through. I've been there. I never met my mother until I was twenty-four. At the age of eight, I was sexually assaulted. My father was an alcoholic. So I know what it's like to feel used, unloved, and unwanted." Donna's past explains why most of her foster children are teenage girls.

Donna endured a new rash of critical remarks when she accepted her first black foster children—a set of five-year-old twin boys. "One neighbor avoided me. Another, I later learned, called me 'white trash.'

"My own Christian walk with the Lord has helped tremendously in my reactions to such comments," Donna continued. "They used to bother me. But now God has given me a certain peace about it. I try to understand why that person said what he did. Often, he knows little about foster care. So I ask God to give him or her a better understanding of the whole foster care program."

From hearing the experiences of many other foster parents like Don and Donna and Mr. and Mrs. B., I learned to place negative responses about foster care into three different categories:

A. *The information-seeking question.* Many people genuinely are interested in learning more about foster care. Interested people most often ask questions like, "How does a child come into foster care?" or, "Do you know how long he (she) will stay with you?" which many times is followed by, 'What are his (her) sizes? I might have some clothes that fit." I can't think of any foster parents who wouldn't gladly answer these types of questions from sincere individuals. But sooner or later most foster parents encounter information-seeking questions from people who desire to learn a few "gory" details about a foster child's background.

One friend of mine has fostered fifty-four babies over the past fourteen years. She says, "When someone makes a comment like, 'It's hard to know the background of an illegitimate child,' I recognize that that person is seeking information. I usually dismiss the remark with a simple, 'I'm satisfied.' After that, most inquisitive people don't know what else to say."

B. *The planned-to-get-a-reaction remark.* Satan knows where we hurt. He knows our vulnerable

NEGATIVE RESPONSES FROM FAMILY AND FRIENDS

spots well. When he uses a hostile or angry person to attack a foster parent's motives ("I'm glad the state pays you a good salary for doing this"), it could be so easy to return a sharp reply. One foster care manual states a solution this way. "Most often if you do not react in the way the other person expects, you are in control of the situation and you 'win.'" Often negative remarks develop simply from a lack of knowledge. If efforts to educate that person fail, Jesus once gave some good advice to His disciples that might also apply here. "And whosoever shall not receive you nor hear your words, when ye depart . . . shake off the dust of your feet" (Matt. 10:14).

C. *The planned-to-get-a-reaction remark made in the presence of the foster parent's children.* These are the same types of remarks explained in the preceding paragraph. Only they are twice as difficult to deal with because of the children's presence. Most parents know their children possess sensitive "radar" tuned to pick up subtle innuendoes between adults in a conversational exchange. Any hint from the foster parent of an unsure position will surely be picked up by his children. Complaints the foster parent has about a foster child or criticisms of the foster care program should be shared privately with the caseworker. Directing complaints elsewhere is like granting permission for others to criticize.

If I received any negative comments as we impatiently waited for our foster care license, they didn't register. My mind seemed to program only the positive, like the conversation I had one Sunday evening with Sister Yvonne, who was one of Jenny's houseparents at the children's home.

"Mrs. Bilow," she said, "you are going to make such a fine foster family. Jenny is so happy. She can't wait to live with you."

"I don't know who's more excited—her or us," I beamed. "There's so much we're trying to accomplish before Jenny's arrival. Time should be going fast, especially with making Christmas preparations too. But it's not. I feel like a little girl who can't wait to open her Christmas packages."

Sister's beautifully plain, large brown eyes gleamed as she laughed. "Maybe the Lord is trying to teach you patience."

"He picked a poor subject, I'm afraid," I returned. "It's taking me a long time to learn."

I was absolutely glowing inside as I walked back to the car. I doubt that any negative comment could have pulled me down—not for long at least. I was high. High on Christ's love for me. He was putting Jenny into our lives. And I nurtured the thought that some day He would give us Jenny—permanently. She would be ours through adoption. Somehow God would perform a miracle. I just knew it.

NEGATIVE RESPONSES FROM FAMILY AND FRIENDS

Hearken unto me, ye that know righteousness, the people in whose heart is my law; fear ye not the reproach of men, neither be ye afraid of their revilings. (Isa. 51:7)

chapter five
Sweet Anticipation

"Have you decided yet?" a store clerk asked for the second time.

Not completely satisfied, I opened each drawer once again. "I'm not certain how much drawer space I'll need." The clerk looked puzzled, and I explained we would soon receive a foster child. I wasn't sure, I told him, how much clothing she had. Surely this piece would accommodate Jenny's wardrobe. And the dresser wasn't too large for the small alcove in which it would fit.

"I'll take it," I replied.

After paying for the dresser and arranging for delivery service, I walked through the store mentally arranging Jenny's bedroom furniture. That large round mirror we had stored someplace several years ago would be perfect right above Jenny's new dresser. Where was it? Still in the attic?

Matt had relinquished his bedroom for Jenny only a week ago. That in itself was a major project. I couldn't help but laugh as I thought about the boys moving Matt's dresser into Mark's room.

"Are you pulling, Matt?" Mark questioned. "It sure doesn't feel like it."

"Well, I've got the heaviest end, you know," nine-year-old Matt replied, somewhat annoyed with his twelve-year-old brother. "Hey, watch that corner, Mark!"

"Don't worry," Mark told him. "Just watch the floor you're scratching up."

The boys finally eased the dresser into the hallway.

"Let's rest a minute, Matt," Mark suggested as he wiped his forehead with the bottom part of his T-shirt.

"Good idea," Matt responded. He dropped to the floor and stretched his limbs in exhaustion after the past fifteen minutes of hard labor.

"I think it would be easier, guys, if you took out all the drawers," I suggested.

"Aw, mom," Mark answered. "That's too much trouble."

"Not in the long run," I told him. Neither made a move to carry out my suggestion.

Two Cokes and a number of cookies later, the boys hoisted the dresser off the floor, ready to continue their short but difficult journey into the next bedroom. Raisin, ever-ready watchdog that she is, was sitting on the sidelines when the doorbell rang. Like a shot she raced through the hallway to announce the caller, tripping Matt along her way. As Matt fell, he tipped the dresser just enough to spill the contents of three drawers. Fruit of the Looms mixed with Viking tube socks donned the floor. Hundreds of pennies which Matt saved in one drawer rolled in every direction, many dropping down the cold-air duct.

"What's going on up there?" Earl bellowed from the basement through the clothes chute. Earl himself literally was elbow deep in a tub of cement. He was mixing mortar to brick up a hearth that would eventually hold a Franklin stove. For the past month, he and the boys had been remodeling the basement—tearing down a wall here and adding a wall there—which ultimately would give us another 400 square feet of living space. Earl wanted so much to complete the new family room in time for Jenny's arrival.

After living in our home for fourteen years, Earl had renovated nearly every room. God truly had given him a special talent—an ability to work well with his hands. Over the years we saved literally many thousands of dollars because of this special gift.

Shopping for Jenny brought twinges of excitement to me as I store-hopped from one girls department to another. Little girls were so much different to shop for. Mark and Matt were "stick straight," so up and down. Jenny was different, more rounded. Her clothes didn't just hang on her the way clothes so often fit the boys. For the first time in my life, I really noticed the difference in shapes of girls as opposed to boys (as silly as that may sound).

While the pressure to complete all these tasks was difficult at times, I believe we also were drawn together as a team. Our family prayers centered around Jenny and the adjustment we all would be making. I prayed for sensitivity to each others' needs and a family unity in His name. To add to the excitement of preparing for Jenny, Christmas was fast approaching. This year truly would bring a double blessing—joy in the birth of Christ our Savior and an opportunity to demonstrate our love for Him by caring for a child separated from her family.

Two of Jenny's sisters had already been placed in foster homes. I was thankful that two sisters rather than one would remain at the children's home once Jenny was placed with us. Both would miss Jenny, but at least they would have each other. No foster homes were available for either one, but we decided to take the girls as often as we could on weekends.

Sandy, our caseworker, had explained to us the night of our home study about the critical shortage of foster homes. Often she contacted social service agencies in neighboring counties because of a lack of homes in her own county. So few homes for such a great need!

I would later learn that frequently broken families who are reunited break again under the strains of daily living pressures, and the children return to foster care (in foster homes or institutions) for another indefinite period of time. Many never return to their natural families.

The consequence of remaining in an in-limbo state, of never having the security of one's own family, was never more clearly impressed upon me than through Casey. Casey struck back—with intensity and fierceness.

But as we prepared for Jenny's arrival, I was totally unaware of the deep-rutted path God would have us follow. Had I known, I believe I would have chosen another.

A man's heart deviseth his way: but the LORD directeth his steps. (Prov. 16:9)

chapter six

And Now We Are Five

The day finally arrived. As I shut the back door, I realized we were leaving our house as a family of four, but would soon return as one of five.

Only a few final touches remained in Earl's beautiful new recreation room. Matt was settled comfortably in Mark's bedroom. Jenny's new dresser, along with the mirror from the attic, fit perfectly in the alcove of Matt's old room. Aside from a few items I knew Jenny needed, the clothes closet was cleared—ready to accommodate her wardrobe. A new bedspread and curtains completed the feminine decor of her bedroom. For a mother who had been totally wrapped up in "boy" things for thirteen years, preparing for Jenny was a delight.

Joyous Christmas music playing on the car radio added to an already exuberant mood as the four of us made the short trip to the children's home. Not only was seven-year-old Jenny being placed in our home in time for Christmas, but her two sisters would spend the holiday with us, too.

As if that wasn't enough excitement, I had just learned the previous day that my sister and her family would be home for Christmas—an event that doesn't happen too often in view of the 2,500 miles between us. My best friend was coming home! We would have so much to share together. Truly the Lord was blessing me that year.

The day we picked up Jenny remains vivid in my memory. The weather was cold, but not a trace of snow lay on the ground.

As we opened the large door to the children's home, once again I read, as I had so many times before, the sign placed near the entrance. It pictured several children walking and playing together and read, "Welcome to our world."

I had already learned about the many dedicated, caring people who surround the children's home: the soft-spoken nuns, who possess a quiet strength that carries them through the most heart-breaking situations; the hundreds of dedicated volunteers, who give anywhere from several hours to several days of their time each week. And people like Bill Slawinski, who gave up a well-paid position in the grocery business to work for a much lower figure as a houseparent for the junior boys.

"Here they are," Sister Mary Ann greeted us with a smile. "Jenny's been waiting for you."

Sister Mary Ann placed a quick phone call to the junior girls department to announce our arrival. Within minutes, Jenny came out carrying a large grocery bag filled with clothes. Sister Yvonne, one of Jenny's houseparents, walked beside Jenny with her arms filled too.

"She's been ready to go since eight this morning," Sister Yvonne laughed.

After Jenny left us to greet the boys, I asked Sister Yvonne how Jenny's two sisters reacted toward her leaving. The girls were so close that I knew Jenny's move into a foster home would be difficult for Brenda, who was then nine, and six-year-old Ann.

"Brenda seemed to accept it," she replied. "But it was hard for Ann. She cried at first. But then she seemed pacified when I told her about spending Christmas with you and still being able to see Jenny during family visits."

My heart went out to Brenda and Ann, whose broken family was being torn apart even more. Ann was so young when all the security she ever knew was swept away from her, leaving her totally lost and confused. Was it any wonder she cried when placed in any new circumstance or environment? Sister Yvonne reassured me that Ann would receive extra doses of tender loving care.

Mark interrupted our conversation as he handed me the Polaroid camera he brought along.

"Mom, take our picture in front of the tree, OK?"

The live Christmas tree was cheerily decorated with small items made by the children and an assortment of store-bought ornaments.

Wearing bib overalls and her long, dark hair straight, Jenny chose not to dress up for her departure from the children's home, thereby looking her natural, tomboyish self. I snapped the picture and sixty seconds later had a reminder of a new dimension added to our lives—one which would ultimately affect many people. The picture—showing Jenny with her arms folded, looking every bit like she had won a much-coveted award in her two newly acquired brothers, Matt displaying his silly mood by sticking out his tongue, and Mark giving the V-for-victory sign over Jenny's head—has come to mean a great deal to me.

By this time Earl had the car packed with three or four boxes and bags, all of Jenny's worldly possessions.

"Ready to go, Jen?" Earl asked her as he came in the door.

She nodded her head and started walking quickly to the door.

"Hey, Jenny," Sister Yvonne called. "Aren't you even going to kiss me goodbye?"

"Oh, I forgot," she replied and hugged Sister tightly.

"You be good, Jen, and come back to see us, OK?" Sister reminded Jenny as she returned the hug.

Jenny clearly was excited about her new home. I marveled at how quickly she wanted to leave behind the past, even though she was also leaving two sisters whom she loved deeply. Would she someday leave me just as quickly?

That night as I drew Jenny's bath water, I

couldn't help but remember our first weekend together at the farm. That night, too, I had prepared her bath water. When it was ready, Jenny stepped into the water and sat with her back to the faucets.

"Why are you sitting that way, Jenny?" I asked. "Why don't you turn around?"

Jenny then crossed her legs and faced the long side of the tub. Amazed, I realized she was totally unfamiliar with a bathtub and didn't know how to sit in one. At the children's home she took showers.

"Have you ever been in a bathtub before, Jenny," I asked. She shook her head.

"How did your mom give you a bath when you were home?"

"She washed us from a pan," Jenny shyly replied.

"All five of you?"

"Uh-huh."

Also during that first weekend at the farm, I noticed Jenny picked up her meat with her fingers and slurped her milk. Her speech was peppered with double negatives and "ain't." Sentences were prefaced with "I want" rather than "may I please have."

Between our working with her on the weekends and her care at the children's home during the week, I could see improvements in some areas of etiquette and speech, but I knew Jenny still needed much more work in both areas. I just knew, though, that Jenny would respond. She wanted to learn. That was so important!

After Jenny's bath her first day in her new foster home, she slipped into a floor-length granny gown that I had recently bought. I brushed her long, dark hair until it gleamed. How special it was to have a little girl.

As I continued to unpack Jenny's clothes she suddenly remembered something and ran out of the room. When she returned, she obviously was hiding something behind her back.

With expectation in her eyes, Jenny handed me a picture of a brightly colored clown. Printed in giant letters was, "I LOVE YOU, MOM AND DAD, FRUM JENNY." My eyes rested on "mom and dad." Jenny loved us enough to want to call us "mom and dad." Tears of joy welled in my eyes.

"I love you, too, Jenny," I said as I hugged her tightly. I silently thanked God for giving us this special opportunity and making us a family of five.

By this shall all men know that ye are my disciples, if ye have love one to another. (John 13:35)

chapter seven
And One More Makes Six

"Lean to the left. Lean to the right. Stand up, sit down, fight, fight, fight!"

Annie, my five-year-old niece from Washington, was teaching Jenny cheerleading routines. Jenny learned quickly.

"Let's do the Viking cheer, Annie!" Their voices joined enthusiastically.

"Hey, all you Viking fans. Stand up and clap your hands. (Clap—clap, clap. Clap—clap, clap.) Now that you're in the beat, this time let's move our feet. (Stomp—stomp, stomp. Stomp—stomp, stomp.) Now that you're in the groove, this time let's really move. (Stomp—clap, clap. Stomp—clap, clap.) Hey, let's move!"

Both girls ended the cheer by sliding easily into splits.

Jenny's natural ability for gymnastic movements was obvious.

Though the two girls had known each other less than a week, a natural rapport had developed between them like that of long-lost friends.

Christmas was very special that year. It was Jenny's first with us. And my sister Carolyn

(Annie's mom) and her family had arrived home. Carolyn and I spent long nights together, playing guitar and singing, catching up on the latest news, and talking about our own personal experiences which, of course, included foster care. Only a month before, Bob and Carolyn had to give up ten-month-old Susan, their first foster child, who had lived with them all but the first eight weeks of her life.

"You wouldn't believe, Pat, how attached to Susan we all were," Carolyn told me during the early morning hours of one such night.

Oh, yes, I could, I thought to myself. I remembered how Carolyn wept so grievously over the phone the day Susan left. It was like a death in the family, she had told me. Danny and Ann felt, too, like they had lost a sister. My brother-in-law Robert felt empty that day when he returned home from work. Susan usually was one of the first persons he greeted.

I recalled how helpless I felt when Carolyn called. With 2,500 miles between us, I could do little but listen to her wracking sobs. Even then, despite her sorrow, she realized Susan was in the Lord's hands—that she had done all she could to give her the best possible beginning in life.

Separation is one of the biggest problems with which foster parents must cope. Many drop out of foster care after the first child because they cannot bear having the child leave, according to one professional in the field. She acknowledges that the first placements are very difficult for foster parents. "You can tell them what it's going to be like when the child leaves. They intellectualize this. But when it comes time for the child to go, emotionally it's a very draining thing."

Foster parents go through mourning when a child leaves. Each copes in a way most comfortable to him or her. Says one foster parent who is a member of a foster parent organization in northwest Ohio, "After having a few children, you develop a habit to help accept separation. I save all my 'busy' work and dig in after each child leaves."

Another member from the same organization says, "Some parents want another child right away. But I need that time just to feel sorry for myself. I need to mourn my loss."

Carolyn too was still mourning her loss. Little Susan had left their care only a month earlier.

"Pat, I can't believe how well Jenny fits in," she abruptly said, changing the subject. Tears welled in her eyes. The emotional wound was still fresh. Healing would take time. "She even looks like Mark and Matt."

That she did, with her brown eyes and dark hair.

"I'd check into a gymnastics class for Jenny," Carolyn continued. "She really has a natural ability. Annie's class has been great for her." I vowed to put that on my list of priorities.

Bob and Carolyn tried to visit as many friends and relatives as possible. During the time they stayed with us, Carolyn tried to keep me informed early in the day about their dinner plans for that evening. Because Mark and Matt were spending some days with Grandma and Grandpa Bilow, our own family was fragmented. And, too, periodically during the holidays, Jenny's two sisters, Brenda and Ann, visited us. Chaotic days, yes. But ones which have since become treasured memories.

Those brief weeks passed swiftly. Bob and Carolyn soon were on their way home. And the dust settled. We stabilized into a comfortable routine. I continued working as a secretary to a corporate officer of a large corporation. Earl was home from his job as an operating engineer with the city before the kids got home from school. I arrived home from work around five each night.

Caring for one more person didn't really seem that much more difficult. Before Jenny came to live with us, I wondered if I would be able to care for another child and still hold my job. But, so far, that didn't pose any problem. It was amazing, though, how God introduced options during the next months that would change the course of our lives.

Two years prior to this time, a tiny seed of interest in writing was just beginning to bear some fruit. This interest, sparked by the completion of a number of journalism night courses, had led me to discuss with professionals in the field the possibility of a career change. The field of journalism, I was told, was extremely competitive. It would be very difficult to break in. Without a college degree, it was practically impossible. But I could try free-lance writing, one journalist suggested.

After covering assignments for several area papers on a gratis basis to acquire experience, I was beginning to receive paid acceptances through the mail from several nonsecular publications. Rejections came by the droves, but each tiny acceptance spurred me on. Discipline in writing (by writing regularly each day) became a way of life for me.

The question I raised to God just prior to attending my first writers conference (Billy Graham's annual Christian School of Writing) was whether He wanted me in the field of writing. The results of the conference resolutely reaffirmed my desire. The question was no longer "Should I write?" but rather "In which area, Lord?"

I can never sufficiently thank well-known professional writers like Margaret Anderson and Ruth Peterman who gave me the reassurance I so needed at that time to build up my confidence. I came back elated. Not only had the Lord directed me into the field of writing, but now He was giving me something to write about! Our next few years in foster care provided a storehouse of experiences from which I still draw.

Many of these involved Jenny. It was so easy to write about her and her progress! What six months in the love of Christ did for Jenny was amazing. Earl and I were committed to a Christian mission outreach for high school students called Young Life. Jenny loved the Young Life activities at our house with the Young Life leaders, club kids, and their spirited guitar-playing and singing. She thrived in the active family environment. We were so pleased with her progress (for example, her bed-wetting stopped completely after she came to live with us) that we toyed with the idea of taking her younger sister Ann.

Once again, the question of working surfaced. I wanted so much to get into the writing field for the company in which I worked, but the doors seemed to be closed. Was God leading me to resign to care for both Jenny and Ann? And what about Brenda, the girls' older sister? If we took Ann, she would be left behind at the children's home.

I prayed in those moments of indecision to ask God to show me His will.

Several weeks later we arranged for Jenny to visit at the children's home all her sisters except the youngest (still a toddler who was living in a foster home).

"Hurry up, Jenny," I said, "or we'll be late."

Jenny was so excited about the visit that she couldn't make a choice between her two best outfits.

"Mom, I don't know which one to wear," she said with a giggle. I could always tell when Jenny was nervous or excited. She giggled.

The trip to the home turned out to be an answer to my prayer. It was such a beautiful spring day that Jenny visited her sisters outside on the home's grounds.

I spotted a woman contentedly sitting on a large wooden swing and asked, "Do you mind if I join you?"

"Not at all," she replied, making room for me.

Our conversation turned toward foster children. I was surprised to learn she was the foster mother to Jenny's oldest sister. She was also a devout Christian. We compared notes about the girls and marveled at how well they fit into our families.

"Patti misses her sisters so much that occasionally we invite Brenda to spend weekends with us," she told me.

"Actually, we've been thinking about taking Ann as a foster child," I said. "But then Brenda would be the only one left here."

"Praise the Lord!" the woman responded with disbelief, joy, and amazement. "My husband and I wanted to take Brenda, but we feared leaving Ann all alone."

I could see God's power and direction working in all our lives! (Eventually all the sisters would be placed in Christian foster homes.)

One month later, we both met again at the children's home—this time to take Brenda and Ann to our respective homes.

As I drove home with the back end of the station wagon loaded with boxes and bags of toys and clothing, amid the kids' excited chatter I mused to myself, And one more makes six. I drew in a deep breath. Thy will be done, Lord.

> Every good gift and every perfect gift is from above, and cometh down from the Father of lights, with whom is no variableness, neither shadow of turning. (James 1:17)

chapter eight
Reassessing Those Priorities!

"OK, girls. Here's what we're going to do."

We were sorting through Ann's belongings. For some reason she had twice as much as Jenny. Finding room for the few things Jenny brought from the children's home was no problem. But now, adding a second child with twice as much as the first meant a little more juggling for space.

"Matt labeled all your dresser drawers for you. Jenny, your name is on the left. Ann, yours is on the right. The labels will help you remember where to put your clothes, OK?"

"OK, mom," Jenny replied, as she neatly placed shirts in a drawer—pleased to have drawers with her own name on them.

"Yes, mom," Ann echoed, following Jenny's example.

Wouldn't it be great if mothers could remind their children only once about a chore and be assured that that responsibility would always be carried out? Jenny and Ann pretty much shared the same view as the boys about household responsibilities—they were a low-priority item.

Eventually we all hit a happy medium. I learned

to relax my attitude toward clutter, and the kids made a better effort to keep things picked up.

Time became a very precious commodity to me. Something always needed to be done. Like Jenny's, Ann's teeth needed immediate attention. She also had an eye disorder which was in the process of being corrected under the supervision of an eye clinic. And, of course, she had to be transferred to our school. Jenny's gymnastics ability was being developed in a class that met three times a week.

With all this plus the boys' activities, Earl and I sometimes felt we spent most of our time inside a car transporting kids back and forth.

When at work, my thoughts were mostly at home. My job no longer seemed exciting. The heavy workload was diversified, and I had enjoyed occasionally traveling for the company to places like New York and Washington. But about the time the girls came into our lives, the excitement connected with working gradually disappeared.

The decision I believe the Lord was leading me to make to leave the company was a difficult one. I began receiving vibrations about my working. Everything I read, various conversations held, people I knew, several incidents, all seemed to lead in one direction—terminate employment.

A struggle weighing the pros and cons of working stretched over the next six months. The loss of my salary most definitely would affect our standard of living. There was a strong probability that my job would be rerated to a higher paying position. Another two and one-half years of service would put me over the ten-year mark, which made me eligible for a pension. Also, the three years I had worked prior to having the children would be reinstated once I achieved those ten years of employment. Gone would be important fringes like dental coverage and eye exams. Surely I could work for just another two and one-half years.

I elaborate about this troubling personal decision for a number of reasons. Too often the tendency to procrastinate is easy. We recognize a problem, inwardly know it should be dealt with, but then procrastinate. For me that problem was security. I didn't want to relinquish material security. To leave the company would mean taking a step in faith—to believe that somehow God would provide not only our material needs but my needs for self-fulfillment as well. When something doesn't feel just right in our lives, when we recognize that a problem or conflict does exist, then I believe God often calls us to action. To procrastinate only prolongs and oftentimes worsens the situation.

Jesus was not a procrastinator. "To day shalt thou be with me in paradise," He told the thief on the cross (Luke 23:43). "Be thou clean," He said, and the lepers were healed (Matt. 8:3). "Go" was His command to the demons. And the two possessed men were freed (Matt. 8:32). "Arise, take up thy bed, and go unto thine house." And the paralytic man walked (Matt. 9:6).

Jesus was a man of instant action. How I admire that! I believe my growing dissatisfaction with my job was His way of calling me to action. But I found it easier to ignore the problem than step out in faith to solve it.

Materialism is a very real problem in today's society. Easy credit enables easy purchases. But behind each purchase are payments. And behind each payment are two or three hidden payments. The extra car needs more insurance, more gas, more maintenance. The cottage or home in the country must be furnished, taxes need be paid, lawn equipment purchased. Two incomes become necessary to make ends meet.

Many women can handle full-time job responsibilities in addition to their home responsibilities. Some really together families are doing remarkable jobs—and growing, too, by working together as a team.

But many others are falling apart, as witnessed over and over again by Judge Andy Devine, who presides over our local court for juvenile offenders. He cites one truancy case typical of untold numbers of others. Seventeen-year-old Sharon was cutting classes to go home early with her friends to drink beer and smoke pot while her mom and dad were working. When Judge Devine suggested to Sharon's mom that she quit her job to spend more time with her daughter, the woman's reply was, "We just bought a new car and a new boat and are heavily mortgaged on our house. I couldn't possibly give up my job."

While mom and dad work their way out of debt, Sharon remains unsupervised at home during a period in her life when her own self-image is probably at one of its lowest ebbs.

"We'd better start denying some of the material well-being that causes some of the problems we are seeing in court today," warns Judge Devine, who presides over many cases involving children in foster care.

I was just as guilty as Sharon's mom regarding materialism. But after a time, I finally recognized what I felt was God calling me to action concerning my job conflicting with our family. I finally resigned the promising career that had once meant so much to me. Doubts permeated my mind after the decision was made—until reassurance came through my exit interview.

I had had a passing acquaintance with the woman who conducted the interview and had always thought well of her. But I didn't know she was a Christian until I noticed a little pin clipped to her "out" basket that read, "Praise the Lord!" We shared comments about our mutual faith. It was easy to confide in her about my nagging fears.

She reaffirmed my decision to leave by saying,

"When God closes one door, Pat, He opens many more." Her warm smile of reassurance left me with renewed confidence of God's providing hand.

How true were her words! Looking back, literally hundreds of doors have been opened since that time. My years of service with the company were excellent preparation for working from my home as a free-lance writer. God not only provided us with a supplemental income through my writing but also allowed me to be a mother who was readily available when needed.

And self-fulfillment? To express my deepest, innermost thoughts and concerns or to capture the very essence of an interview with someone in a business management position for all the world to read—now that's self-fulfillment!

Since being separated from my job, I now realize I was giving the best part of myself not to my family, but to a corporation. The better time of my waking hours was devoted to the company, as was the best part of my personality. The leftovers went to my family.

Had it not been for Jenny and Ann's entrance into our lives, I might yet be locked into a position in which my writing, a gift from God, would not have been developed. The experience of serving the Lord as a foster family would not have added a new dimension to our lives. This book would not exist. The placement of all five sisters in Jenny's family in Christian homes may not have occurred. And, most importantly, the girls may not have grown in their Christian faith or witnessed to their mother.

Had the girls not reached her, would someone else have tried to bring her the message of salvation? Would she have listened to anyone else? Only the Lord knows.

> I will instruct thee and teach thee in the way which thou shalt go: I will guide thee with mine eye. (Ps. 32:8)

chapter nine
Adjusting to Special Problems

Jenny adapted to our family unit with relative ease. Ann did too, six months later, but I doubt the transition would have been as smooth had it not been for Jenny's presence.

As my sister said, their brown eyes and dark hair made the girls look like Mark and Matt's natural sisters. Those who didn't know our family thought they were. And I finally had the little girls I always wanted—definitely a wrong motive for getting into foster care. (But I believe here is a perfect example in which the Lord, in His timing, used a wrong motive to bring about glory to His name.)

It didn't take Mark long to get over his puppy love for Jenny. About three weeks, and the honeymoon was over. (Authorities say the "honeymoon period" generally lasts from one to three months. The child then begins to relax in his new setting and be himself.)

"Mom, she did it again! Jenny broke the string on my yo-yo."

"No, I didn't."

"Don't lie, Jenny. You did too!"

"I did not."

"Yes, you did."

While I was in the bathroom fixing my hair for a dinner meeting, the bickering continued. Finally I laid down the curling iron.

"All right, you two. Let's get to the bottom of this."

We sat on Jenny's bed as Mark told his side of the story. Earlier that day he had put his yo-yo on top of the stereo speaker in his bedroom. Later it was gone. A search uncovered the toy, with a broken string, under the davenport. Jenny stood to defend herself.

"I haven't seen Mark's yo-yo all day. I didn't take it."

"Are you sure, Jenny?" I questioned.

She nodded her head.

Matt and Ann had been gone since Mark first placed the yo-yo on his stereo, which automatically made them not guilty.

"Jen, be truthful," I said. Jenny had lied to us before, and I sensed she was not telling the truth again. "Look straight in my eyes."

She turned her head toward me.

"Have you seen it, honey?" I asked softly.

She looked at me, her eyes filling with tears. She was becoming visibly upset.

"I didn't take it," she answered shakily as she started to cry. She threw herself down on the bed and sobbed, "I want my mom!"

Her plea startled me. For an instant I had forgotten that I wasn't her natural mother.

I signaled Mark to leave. As he slipped out, he closed the door behind him. I picked up Jenny and held her close in my arms.

"It's OK, Jenny, you don't need to cry anymore," I whispered, gently stroking her hair away from a tear-stained face. "No need to cry, honey. It's all right."

We sat together quietly until her tears subsided into an occasional sob. How difficult it must be, I thought, for her not to be with her family! To have to live with strangers who have an entirely different set of values. Whose ways of communicating with each other are so different from her family's!

I tried to explain to Jenny why lying was deceitful. "Sometimes it's easier for us to tell a little white lie to cover up something wrong we've done. It's really hard to tell the truth knowing sometimes we have to suffer the consequences. But lying hurts others. And worse yet, we hurt ourselves.

"God asks us to love one another as ourselves. That's something we can't do when we lie. Lies can build, Jenny. We start out with one small lie. The next one is a little easier to tell. The third is easier still and the fourth a little bigger, until finally people don't know when to believe us. Do you understand, Jenny?"

"Yes," she answered in a soft voice.

"Jenny," I said still holding her. "I'm going to ask you just once. And I will believe whatever you tell me. Did you take Mark's yo-yo?"

"Yes, but I didn't mean to break the string." She could barely be heard as she turned her head toward the floor.

Squeezing her tightly, I said, "Thank you, Jenny, for telling the truth."

I wish I could say that was the end of Jenny's lying, but it wasn't. It took a long time for her to break the habit. Actually, she never did completely. But by the time she left us, her tendency to lie had greatly decreased.

Through contact with other foster parents and caseworkers, I've found lying and stealing to be one of the most common problems associated with foster children. This is not to imply that other children never lie or steal. Most do—at least during some period of their lives. But it seems to be more prevalent among homeless children.

Perhaps this is because many come into foster placement with deficits in various areas of their lives. (That's what is so great about foster care! It gives believers the opportunity to offer fulfillment through the gospel of Jesus Christ. And what better way than through a child who is still pliable and not hardened by the problems of life!)

Certain needs foster children have as human

beings have not been met adequately. One of the lower level, basic needs is food. A good example of this was told to me by a caseworker from the Midwest. One of her cases involved a foster child who came from a background in which there never was enough food. Consequently, that child became fearful about not having enough food. He even resorted to stealing and hoarding food to meet this primary need.

When basic material and physical needs are met, the child moves on to fill his needs for friendships and self-confidence, according to the caseworker. After these are attained, he seeks higher level experiences of love, intimacy, and self-fulfillment. The process is much like Maslow's hierarchy of human needs.

Jenny was basically a well-adjusted child, more so, I later learned, than her sisters. This short essay she wrote in second grade told me a lot about her feelings:

> Spring is when the birds sing and when the wedding bells ring. I like Spring because that's the time when flowrs start to hatch. If you want to learn more about Spring, go and smell the air and find out. But some flowrs don't even get looked at.

Sometimes flippant on the outside, she revealed through her composition a real sensitivity on the inside.

About a year after she moved in, Jenny asked Mark to take her picture in an already-too-small, two-piece bathing suit. I couldn't help but remember when she first came how extremely shy she was, even fearful, that someone might see her in her underpants, or worse yet, nude. I attributed this to the fact that she never had any brothers around and was being very cautious. But when she realized Mark and Matt had every intention of respecting her privacy, she relaxed her fears.

Jenny was five when she was taken from her mother. Ann was four. Maybe that one year made the difference. Or perhaps Ann was a little more dependent than Jenny. But Ann seemed to have more difficulty coping with the separation from her mother.

When Ann came to us, any new surroundings or situations frightened her. In these instances she would cling to Earl and me almost like another layer of skin. One holiday weekend was particularly upsetting for her. She cried the night we had dinner with my in-laws. The next morning in church she cried. And the tears continued to flow that afternoon when we visited my parents. Her crying stopped only when I would hold and comfort her in my arms.

Gradually, though, as she became more familiar with us and our circle of friends and relatives, she relaxed.

Shirley Stretchbery, the supervisor of our county's foster homes department, whom I quoted earlier, made these comments to me once. "Trying to understand the whole family communication system is very difficult for the foster child. And the foster family doesn't understand some of the actions of the foster child. The natural children think fostering is beautiful at first. But then they realize it's cutting into their time."

Says one foster mother of a sixteen-year-old girl, "When I felt my own children were struggling, I worried at times if they needed to be put through this and if the lessons in the long run were going to pay off. I'm hoping they will. But I have had to reinforce very strongly with my children that I do love them and that fostering is not a choice between them and our foster daughter."

Mark and Matt, too, occasionally felt jealousy and resentment toward their foster brothers and sisters. It was difficult for them to understand why Ann was so upset that holiday weekend. They felt she was vying for our attention.

But every family has its own unique character or style. And Ann wasn't yet familiar with ours. Your family's communication system is to some degree different from every other family's system. When one stops to consider how extremely complex relationships are in this system, is it any wonder foster parents should be prepared for some rough going when adding a new member?

Especially one from a completely different family system that may have an entirely different set of values?

Foster kids' lives are unique. Being placed in foster care is a critical event most children never forget. It is an experience with built-in difficulties. The foster child encounters three unique experiences:
1. Being moved from one life style into another which often conflicts with his or her own;
2. Living in a strange home, with strangers, in a different physical setting, going to a strange school, adapting to strange discipline, life style and values; and
3. Having two sets of parents at one time (although many children are experiencing this as a result of divorces and remarriages).

(In addition, the physical separation from his family makes him feel he has lost his identity. Foster parents can help overcome this by encouraging him to keep mementos from his life prior to placement and by providing possessions of his own.)

So in this day of rising family turmoil, economic instability, and a me-oriented society, who in the world wants to undertake more potential problems by becoming foster parents? Believe it or not, thank God, many beautiful, concerned people. (But not as many as there once were, according to every caseworker I interviewed. An increasing number of women are in the work force.)

What successful combination of ingredients makes a foster family work well? Most certainly, all members of the family must be in total agreement about accepting the responsibilities of foster care. And, most certainly, the marriage itself should be strong, with both parents working together as a team. (Because of the foster child's need for a two-parent family, it is difficult for a single individual to become licensed as a foster parent.)

Marilyn Compton, supervisor of foster care for a Catholic social service agency, expressed these thoughts as well. "Foster parents must have a real love for kids. And they should be flexible, especially in what they expect from a child.

"Rewards may be very, very small. Maybe in the short time they have the child, he's stopped most of his lying. Or he remembers to brush his teeth without being told. Possibly, his grade card contains one *D* instead of all failures.

"Foster parents must have the ability to roll with the punches and be willing to invest a whole lot of themselves and their time."

Perhaps social workers should forewarn prospective foster parents about some of the dangers involved, although I think we tend to underestimate the depth of strength the Lord gives us when we need it most. (One foster parent friend of mine feels licenses should be awarded only after completion of orientation courses in addition to regular requirements.)

Faith can be a great shock absorber. I believe there are some situations no amount of course work can prepare one for. How could our caseworker have prepared us for Casey's vandalism act—an act no social service agency in our area had ever before experienced? How can a foster parent be prepared for accusations of child abuse brought against him or her by the natural parent? How does one prepare to let go? Especially when the child is older and has been in placement for a long period?

It is interesting to note here that separation is not always a sad time. Says one joy-filled Christian mother who fosters babies, "Once in a while God drops a real grouch our way. I think He does this to make sure we don't get too high and mighty. He wants us to remember not to be possessive."

Nevertheless, separation remains to be one of the primary reasons why many drop out of the foster parent ranks.

Coping with natural parent visitations is another reason why some foster parents elect to leave. Today's society is very much "rights" oriented—civil rights, women's rights, the rights of the physically and mentally handicapped, and, most recently, the rights proposed in the International Year of the Child.

Natural parents who have children in foster

care placement are becoming more aware of their parental rights. In our county, natural parents are allowed a minimum of one visit a week with their children if they so choose. Visitations can be upsetting for both the child and the foster parents. (The natural parents usually do not visit with their child in the foster home, but rather in a predetermined neutral area such as the social service agency office.)

But these visits are very much necessary. The purpose of foster family care is to provide a temporary home for children separated from their parents and to reunite those children as quickly as possible with their natural parents. The visits with the natural parents not only help maintain the relationships between the child and the parents but they also keep the child in touch with reality.

Without the visits, the child can form unrealistic, glorifying pictures of the natural parents and their experiences as a family. Eventually, the child can replace reality with his imagined pictures. Foster parents should be prepared for mixed feelings on their part toward the natural parents. Conversely, the natural parents experience much the same types of feelings toward the foster parents. Often, there are elements of jealousy and conflict.

Foster parents also break away from fostering as a result of unacceptable behavior on the child's part (such as lying, stealing, use of profanity, or alcohol and drug use). Some become frustrated because of their inability to change the child's behavior in a relatively short time.

Says one caseworker, "A child who has been using profanity for several years is not going to change in two or three months."

Foster parents should be made aware of the possibility of these conflicts, although most are never exposed to extremes in behavior like compulsive stealing or use of drugs or alcohol. Those who would be frightened away by these possibilities probably shouldn't be in foster care anyway.

Successful foster parenting is accomplished by those who have a real love for children and are not necessarily doing it as a "good work." Often, fostering fills a need. It could be the "empty nest" depression experienced by the middle-aged mother. Or maybe the need to share what one has with another. Or perhaps it is the need of an adult like Mr. B. or Donna Harbison who grew up in foster care and knows first hand the feelings experienced by a foster child.

These very real needs are met by the foster child because of the commitment the foster parent makes to that child. Each step of progress, no matter how small, can be gratifying to the committed foster parent. And for the committed Christian foster parent, watching a child's spiritual growth can be the ultimate!

ADJUSTING TO SPECIAL PROBLEMS

Jenny and Ann had already received some Christian training from the children's home before they came to live with us. But to watch them grow even more was exciting. Happiness for Jenny, Ann, and myself was praying together every night. I think they loved as much as I did our nightly ritual of "tucking in," which we preceded by a few songs on the guitar. One of the girls' favorites was, "I Wish We'd All Been Ready," written by Larry Norman, a popular American folk singer, and based on Matthew 24:40-44.

Singing was "sissy stuff," according to Mark and Matt (at least, my kind of singing). As the boys grew older, they preferred to pray by themselves. Understandably so, it was particularly gratifying to me to have two beautiful girls like Jenny and Ann show an interest in "my" kind of music and actually not feel right about going to sleep at night until each of us prayed together.

While Mark and Matt needed fewer of mom's hugs and kisses, Jenny and Ann welcomed them. And often initiated some of their own.

The girls did, indeed, fill a void in my life.

If any of you lacks wisdom, let him ask God, who gives to all men generously and without reproaching, and it will be given him. But let him ask in faith, with no doubting, for he who doubts is like a wave of the sea that is driven and tossed by the wind. (James 1:5-6 RSV)

chapter ten

Family Ties That Bind

"A couple more days of this kind of weather, and the rink will be ready," Earl said as he sipped a hot cup of coffee. He looked out the kitchen window into the side lot. An ice skating rink he and the boys made had just a few more rough spots to be worked out. The kids' anticipation grew more each day.

The cold weather held. Saturday morning, all four kids excitedly got into skates and winter gear to try out the new rink, which finally was ready.

Ann was worried. "I don't know how to skate," she moaned.

"I don't even have skates," Jenny countered.

"I'll teach you how," Matt told Ann eagerly. "And Ruth Ann said she's got an old pair of skates for you, Jenny."

Ten-year-old Ruth Ann lived two houses down the street. She, along with her parents and brother, had taken a special interest in the girls. Ruth Ann's mother, Jean Montaine, often gave us good clothes that her daughter had outgrown (as did several other friends and relatives). Although we did have a small clothing allowance for the girls, the donations helped cut down expensive purchases from a store.

Mark and Matt helped the girls find warm winter gear to wear. Soon the four of them—bundled to their eyeballs—were on the ice, laughing over every spill they took. Raisin, our dog, playfully tugged on whoever happened to be sprawled on the ice as if to say, "Come on. Get up!"

"Let's play a game of tag," Mark suggested.

"But I'll never be able to catch anyone," Ann cried as she hobbled around on her skates.

"Here," Mark replied. "Use this." He gave her part of an old broom stick to help her keep in balance.

Jenny was beginning to glide on the ice now with more confidence.

Though it was cold, the sun was brightly shining. Up in my office at the head of the stairs, I was trying to complete a writing assignment. The office was very small, no bigger than eight feet square. But with large windows on two sides, it was perfect for my needs. My very own room with plenty of light, a desk, used IBM Executive typewriter, filing drawers, and a wooden cabinet Earl had made for supplies. A place to think, pray, and write.

But that day I was having a difficult time doing any of those things. It was more fun to watch the kids and snap some pictures. The pictures could be used with several devotions I was writing.

"OK, kids. Lunch time." I had finished shooting a roll of black-and-white film and had soup and hot chocolate on the stove. The kids came tromping in covered with snow.

"Brush off your suits with a broom first before you come in," I instructed while dishing up the soup. "Jenny, we've got to get you to gymnastics in exactly forty-five minutes. Not much time."

"I'll hurry, mom," she replied.

My sister Carolyn's earlier observation proved correct. Jenny was a natural. Her teacher, a Bulgarian refugee who excelled as a gymnastics instructor, placed Jenny in a special class that received additional time twice a week. In the larger group, Ann also participated.

I loved to watch Ann. While Jenny was the epitome of grace, Ann was almost the opposite. Somehow, she always rolled a little too far left when doing somersaults. Or she'd turn lickety-split cartwheels. While Jenny might be a Snow White or Cinderella, Ann was Winnie the Pooh. She had an inner beauty uniquely her own. She made you want to reach out and hug her just because she tried a little harder.

When Ann came to live with us, she was almost legally blind. The children's home discovered she had amblyopia (lazy eye). To strengthen her bad eye, she wore a patch on her good eye. Biweekly trips to a clinic showed slow but steady improvement.

Ice skating, gymnastics, the trips to the eye clinic—all became threads of activity that were woven into the patterns of our lives. Including the dreaded clothes shopping.

The vouchers authorizing purchases of specific items of clothing tend to further remind the foster child that he is different. First, sales clerks have a difficult time deciphering the vouchers. When they finally do understand, the manager of the department must be called to approve the purchase. By this time, ten other people are waiting to pay for their purchases—most of whom are projecting looks of dismay because they think you are one of those "welfare people" living off their tax dollars. The situation is further provoked when you short-hand the department because one of the clerks must walk you and the child to the credit department to verify the charge account and ring up the bill.

By the end of the whole procedure, foster parent and child feel like crawling in a small hole and eating a can of worms.

Though the girls saw their mother about once a month, up to this point they seldom talked about going home. For some time, their father had made no attempt to see them. It was as if we all felt deep inside they would be with us permanently.

Kay Crawford, who replaced Sandy our original caseworker, had even approached us about the possibility of adoption.

"We plan to seek permanent custody," she told us one day. "We need to determine the possibility of permanent placement to include in the records going to the court. Are you willing to adopt either one or both the girls?"

I couldn't believe what I was hearing. The girls might be ours—permanently!

Of course, my answer was yes when she called back. And perhaps that's exactly what it was—my answer. Earl said he wanted to adopt them, but I remember wondering at the time if he consented because he knew how much I wanted the girls. Mark and Matt approved after some hesitation. Permanent sisters were a different matter than temporary ones.

The long winter that year slowly crept into spring. We had heard nothing for two or three months about the court date which would decide whether parental rights would be terminated. Finally, one dismal rainy day the phone rang. It was Kay Crawford.

"Pat, there's been some changes in our case," she said. "It's almost unbelievable. The mother has found a house."

That had been one of the biggest stumbling blocks in our favor. Before the children could be reunited with their mother, she had to have a suitable house.

"How did that happen?" I asked in amazement. My hand trembled as I held the phone. The girls' mother had been remarried for over a year. Her new husband had been laid off work for quite some time. I knew they were having a difficult time maintaining even their small apartment above a garage. To find, move into, and maintain a house seemed at the most a very remote possibility.

But since our last conversation with Mrs. Crawford, a series of events had taken place. The judge for the case became ill, she told me. This created a large backlog of cases, which bought the girls' mother and her husband additional time.

Mrs. Crawford continued, "The husband was called back to work. They are paying off their bills, and, amazingly enough, someone has offered the couple free occupancy of a large farmhouse with the stipulation that they renovate it."

Though the girls knew none of these things, they suddenly began talking about their mother and sisters and the possibility of once again living together.

The handwriting was on the wall. But I fully refused to accept any of it. In the end God would come through to provide what was best for everyone. And, after all, wasn't living with us in relative comfort, which included gymnastic lessons and Christian training, in their best possible interests?

About this same time, I invited the girls' oldest two sisters and their foster parents to our house for a visit. Since our first chance meeting that day at the children's home, we had kept in contact. John and Joy Miller were Christian fundamentalists. The way they seemed to totally rely on Christ made me feel that somehow they had an inside hotline to heaven.

Joy earlier had told me how remote the possibilities were for them to adopt their very first foster child. All the evidence pointed toward the girl returning to her natural parents. Both Joy and John prayed earnestly about the situation. Through a strange set of events, soon the child was theirs to adopt.

That's how it would happen to us. Somehow God would make the impossible possible. I was excited about the Millers' visit. We could pray about the girls together. Their "connections" with God would provide a solid reinforcement. I knew God listened to me. But somehow, having their support would be reassuring.

As I turned down the Sloppy Joes to simmer, the doorbell rang. Raisin barked and the girls jumped up and down excitedly.

"They're here! They're here! Let's hide."

"No, Ann. That's silly," Jenny replied.

The girls looked forward to these reunions with great anticipation. Though all four sisters were shy at first, it didn't take long for quiet reluctance to give way to noisy familiarity. And, then, Mark and Matt proved to be an added attraction for the two older sisters, Patti and Brenda.

With dishes finished and the kids playing outside, the four of us had a chance to talk with a minimum of interruptions.

"I'm really concerned about the possibility of the girls returning to their mother," I said, opening the conversation.

"John seems to feel that this is what the Lord wants," Joy replied.

I turned to her in disbelief.

"Why do you feel that way, John?" Earl asked.

"Patti and Brenda have been witnessing to their mother every time they see her," he replied. "And she has been listening. The Lord may want to use these girls to bring her to Him. I just have a feeling He wants this family to be reunited."

I felt a large portion of my support crumble. Was I standing alone? Earl kept his thoughts to himself. The girls continued to talk more about their mother and sisters. Mark and Matt even made a few affirmative comments about the family living together. And now the Millers.

But surely God and I were a majority.

In the multitude of my thoughts within me
thy comforts delight my soul. (Ps. 94:19)

chapter eleven
"Why, God?"

It was an unseasonably hot, muggy spring morning when the phone rang.

"Hello?" Matt answered. "Just a minute, please. Mom, it's for you. Mrs. Crawford. Hurry up!"

"Yes, Mrs. Crawford," I responded with anticipation. Had the hearing been held? Did the county receive permanent custody? Was she going to say the girls were now adoptable?

"The Welfare Department has decided to award the girls to their mother on a trial basis," she continued.

There it was—the news I inwardly feared for so long.

Sensing my despair, she added, "We are going to closely monitor the situation. If we find any indications that it isn't working, yours will be the first family to be considered for replacement."

The remainder of our conversation centered on departure details. Someone would pick up the girls in three weeks. Would I please make sure that all records and report cards were included in their belongings?

"It's going to be hard, I know," she said sympathetically. "But you and Earl can rest assured that you have done a beautiful job. The girls have made amazing progress."

But there's so much more to be done, I thought agonizingly.

Mrs. Crawford said she would reconfirm the arrival time a day or two in advance. I went up to my office to think and pray through the situation. I knew intellectually that no child ultimately belongs to his parents. Whether that child is born to his parents, adopted by parents, or placed into the home of foster parents, he is not their property.

Rather he is a gift from God. The girls had been placed in our care for twelve and eighteen months. Was the purpose of their placement so that they might be nurtured in their Christian faith? That they might eventually lead their mother in her own Christian walk?

Earl's response to the news was more out of concern for me. The next day he sent me fifteen beautiful yellow roses, one for each year of our marriage. Mark and Matt accepted the news well. ("We knew it was coming, mom.")

And now we had another member of the family to consider—Grandpa Bilow. A month earlier grandma blessedly died after a six-week-long, debilitating illness. Four days after her funeral, grandpa suffered a tragic fall. He had decided to fix a leak in his garage roof, probably in an effort

"WHY, GOD?"

to forget that that particular day was Mother's Day. The wind caught the garage door. It blew open and knocked his ladder out from under him. Grandpa fell about twelve feet to concrete pavement. In addition to the emotional suffering of losing his wife of fifty-four years, he now would suffer physical pain, with a knee injury, cracked ribs, a broken arm and nose, multiple abrasions, and a very swollen, black-and-blue face.

It seemed almost too much for one man to bear. Yet it proved to be the perfect time for this seventy-nine-year-old man to think about his relationship with the Lord. After a two-week hospital stay, grandpa moved in with us for eight weeks of recuperation. The dining room was converted to a makeshift bedroom. The boys offered him their bedroom, but grandpa could not yet climb steps.

I introduced him to daily devotions. For the first time ever, we prayed together. Tears came to his eyes that beautiful summer morning outside after our prayer. Since then, we have experienced a new depth in our relationship, as I believe he has with the Lord.

Grandpa and the girls had always enjoyed each other. But now what chance would they have to expand their friendship?

Mrs. Crawford advised us to use our own judgment as to when we should tell the girls about their new home. Earl and I decided to break the news after dinner one night.

"We've got a surprise for you, Jenny and Ann," Earl said. Both turned expectantly to him.

"What is it, dad?" Ann asked eagerly.

"You're going home soon with your mother and sisters," he answered.

"You're kidding," Jenny responded.

"With Patti, Brenda, and Kathy?" Ann asked.

"No, we're not kidding," I chimed in. "Yes, Ann, with Patti, Brenda, and Kathy."

"I don't believe it," Ann cried, a wary smile beginning to cross her face.

"It's true, Ann," Matt told her. "You really are going home."

Ann finally believed what she probably had wanted to hear for the past four years.

"Did you hear that, Jenny? We're going to live with mom!" She grabbed Jenny by the arms and started to twirl her around the kitchen.

"Stop it, Ann!" Jenny burst into tears.

Ann quickly released her.

"What's wrong, honey?" I asked, facing Jenny with my hands on her shoulders.

"I don't want to leave you and dad," she cried, tears streaming down her cheeks.

I pulled her into my arms. "Jenny, Jenny. This isn't a time to be sad, honey. You're finally going to be a family again. Just think, you'll be living with your sisters. You girls can pitch in and help your mom. And you'll have all kinds of room outside to play because you'll be living on a farm."

"I'll bet your mom and new stepdad will even have a dog and maybe a few kittens," Earl added.

Jenny's spirits were beginning to lift.

"Maybe they'll even buy us a pony, Ann!" she said, her excitement mounting. She turned to Ann, whose own initial joy was now turning to sadness.

"Why are you crying, Ann?" Mark asked her.

"Now I don't want to leave," she wept.

The girls ran an emotional seesaw during the next several hours. One minute they were sad, the next, happy. Soon, we were all laughing. By bedtime the paradoxical mood swings had stabilized.

As they prepared for bed, the girls seemed excited about the prospect of returning home.

"Check me, mom," Ann said as she hopped in the bottom berth of the bunk bed. "I didn't forget to wash my elbows or brush my teeth."

"Very good, Ann!" I told her after concluding an elaborate inspection that included a few tickles. Jenny had been unusually quiet, lying in bed as though she were struggling with a problem.

"I've got it," she said suddenly, popping up from under the covers.

"Got what, Jen?" I asked.

"The answer to how we can live with you and my mom."

"Oh, and how is that?"

"My mom and new stepdad and our sisters can live here in the attic! It's big, and we can get it all cleaned up," Jenny responded excitedly. I chuckled to myself, thinking how simple a child's solution can be to a complex problem.

The feelings I had over the next several weeks bothered me. But after talking with a number of other foster parents and social workers, I have found they were normal. Often, when foster parents really accept an impending separation, they start withdrawing their feelings for the child to protect themselves from hurt. Emotionally for the foster parent, separation from a meaningful relationship means death. And death means grieving.

Mary Reistroffer, author for the Child Welfare League of America, Inc., points out in a booklet entitled *What You Always Wanted to Discuss About Foster Care But Didn't Have the Time or the Chance to Bring Up* that pulling back feelings can be a danger point. If the regular flow of feelings and attention normally directed to the foster child is diminished or, worse yet, discontinued, the child may react in adverse ways. He may regress to bed-wetting or unwanted behavior, or become physically ill. His new beginning with his natural parents could be in danger of a poor start. And, adjustment problems when reuniting a number of siblings who have been exposed to varying degrees of social incomes and levels is a difficult problem in itself.

A foster child needs to know he is leaving with the foster parents' blessings—that the foster parents are not brushing him off or having him removed from their home because they don't love him.

In the time we had the girls, washing, folding clothes, and picking up after and cooking for two extra people didn't seem like that much extra work. Now that I knew the girls were leaving, I started to look forward to having more room in the house, extra time to myself, and eating out more often. I accepted, maybe for the first time, that these children were not mine. Though I still loved them, my feelings for them were somehow different. I began divorcing myself from them. I thought I would never see them again.

The day came quickly. Boxes, bags, and suitcases were neatly stacked by the front door. I made one last tour through the house to make sure nothing was left behind.

The girls' bedroom looked starkly empty now. One last check under the bed. A pair of flowered underpants. Down to the living room. Nothing behind the piano or under the furniture. Winding my way through the dining room (now grandpa's bedroom) into the kitchen, I spotted in a corner on the floor a plastic ring one of the girls got from the dentist. A few more articles were picked up in the laundry and recreation rooms. I didn't want anything left behind. It would only serve as a reminder.

The girls were waiting patiently on the front porch steps to be picked up. They had said their goodbyes earlier to Earl before he had left for work. The boys were on a canoe trip and had bid the girls well before they left.

"She's here! She's here!" Ann called excitedly as a small station wagon pulled up in front of our house.

Jenny threw her arms around grandpa and gave him a kiss. "Goodbye, grandpa," she said. Touched by her unexpected gesture, he returned her hug and wished her and Ann well.

The girls quickly started carrying their belongings to the car. They almost couldn't wait to leave.

"Goodbye, mom," Jenny said hurriedly.

"Be good, girls," I told them, setting the last bag in the car. "Help your mom." One quick hug and kiss and they were gone—waving enthusiastically as they rode down the street. Not even so much as an "I love you," I thought to myself. Why, God? Why did they have to leave?

Tears wouldn't come. I wandered down the street to see Jean Montaine. She had grown to be a good friend, always ready to listen and share any current problems of the day. Restless, though, I soon came home and headed for my office.

Writing was the perfect release.

Fear thou not; for I am with thee: be not dismayed; for I am thy God: I will strengthen thee; yea, I will help thee; yea, I will uphold thee with the right hand of my righteousness. (Is. 41:10)

chapter twelve
A Prompt Answer Plus Bonus!

God's timing is nothing short of perfect! The annual Billy Graham Christian School of Writing happened to be scheduled only two weeks before the girls left us.

At the conference I was overwhelmed by the multitude of options open to the committed writer—options which could be used either directly or indirectly to glorify Him. Upon talking with a number of longtime professionals in various fields of writing, I felt the Lord's affirmation in the direction that my life was taking. To underestimate the dimension of a talent given by the Lord would be an excuse not to work hard to develop that gift.

The input from the conference took months to digest. It was the perfect outlet to soften the blow of separation. A time to be alone. A time for growing. A time to learn.

Upon our minister's recommendation, two months later I attended another writers conference near Chicago. This one, sponsored by an insurance company affiliated with the synod of our church, made me aware of the great need for writers within our own synod. So many doors being opened! And only a year earlier I had terminated full-time employment—the wiseness of which I was only beginning to experience.

Surrounded by God's love emanating from people I had never known before, at the end of an unforgettable week I was finally able to release the pent-up sorrow I felt toward losing the girls.

Prior to the conference, Jenny and Ann had been gone only five weeks when another phone call came from Mrs. Crawford.

"The children's home is closing its senior boys department," she explained. "We have a fourteen-year-old boy who needs a family environment. I think you and Earl would be great for him." Casey, she told us, had four brothers and sisters. His parents were divorced. In spite of many promises made by his mother, it didn't appear as though she'd ever be in a position to care for all her children.

While I was attending the writers workshop near Chicago, Casey came to live with us. This time Earl handled the physical details of moving. That Saturday morning, he and the boys came to Chicago to pick me up. With them were Casey and nine-year-old Julie, a girl from the children's home who was visiting us for the weekend.

Skinny as a rail, Casey was built just like Mark. "Casey, you look familiar," I said after we greeted.

"I know," he replied with a smile. "I spent a

weekend with you at your farm a couple years ago."

"Remember, mom?" Mark added. "We went to the fair that weekend."

"That's right," I recalled. "Now I remember Casey!"

The boys helped carry my luggage to the van. Casey took my guitar. "I play guitar, too," he told us proudly.

"Oh, no," Mark exclaimed kiddingly, slapping his hand to his face. "Now we've got two in the family to listen to."

Earl and I laughed. So far Casey and Mark were getting along well. But would it last? Especially when sharing the same bedroom offered little privacy for either one?

Professionals in the field of foster care agree that teenagers are the most difficult age group to place. The physical and psychological changes they undergo are bound to spell occasional upheavals within their family units. Self-images can reach all-time lows during these years. But the foster teenager copes not only with this emotionally bumpy ride into adulthood, but with the separation from his natural family as well. More than at any other age, the foster teenager needs a sense of belonging—an identity of his own.

Though Casey had been separated from his family for three years, he still clung to his dream of someday being reunited. Through the years, he had reacted as many foster children do. He began to glorify a very negative family situation. We didn't really understand the depth of his dream until after he was gone. Left behind was a diary in which Casey revealed his innermost feelings— feelings which he held deep inside.

But for a while at least, Casey blossomed in a family environment even though it was not his own. Perhaps at this point he felt fortunate. While he was enjoying a one-to-one relationship with a "normal" family, most of the other boys he had lived with were being transferred to other institutions.

I think, too, that Casey's positive attitude made the smooth transition possible. We had his full cooperation. He wanted a successful placement. So, consequently, at that point it was. Later a number of negative experiences would make Casey change his attitude. He would no longer want to live with us. And he would make sure that we no longer wanted him to live with us.

Even though I had Casey and a variety of writing projects to occupy my time, I couldn't help but think of the girls. Mail time was an important part of my day. Included in the daily mail could be a new writing assignment, publication of an article, or occasionally a check.

Quickly thumbing through the usual assortment of bills and advertisements one day, I came across a letter addressed to Earl and Pat Bilow.

A PROMPT ANSWER PLUS BONUS!

The return address indicated the letter was from the girls. Shaking with excitement, I opened it.

Hi there.
How have you been. I hope fine. Mark and Matt, are you still there? Good, you are. Remeber, I still love you. I miss you. Hay! Mark. Patti likes you very much. Do you like her? She would like to hear from you. Soon. Tell Matt to write me. I would like to hear from him too. I love you all. By now. Right soon.

Love,
Jenny

Written on the envelope was "God Bless Ya All." The envelope obviously had been addressed by Jenny's mother. For the first time I had a different feeling for this woman. She actually was allowing us to have contact. I thought I'd never see or hear from the girls again.

A month later we received this letter with no greeting or closing, but written in Jenny's handwriting:

I stood outside the pearly gates of Hevean, Jesus was inside. then I saw Angels robed in white. I new I'd seen those little faces somewhere befor. I reconnized my 5 little girls. and thue I stood in tears, like a stranger at the door. I had no money, I had no friends. Then my little girls called out to me, 'Daddy won't you come on it.' they seid we've waited oh so long, and now your finally here. Daddy look! these streets are paved with gold, and we got a mancion. there it sits right over there. Daddy wotes taking you so long? arn't you glad to see us agein. I sure wish you would hurry up, and come on in! Then the lord looked at me and there was a pity in his eyes, as he seid, son, I've trid to tell oh so many times, but you just wouldn't listen. and now you've lived your life in sin. then I heard my little girls call out say hay Daddy won't you come on in? I turned my face away from them, and I geuss they must of just stood there and cried. so the lord put his armes around my little girls and seid, Childern your Daddy can't come in.

I never learned where Jenny got this or who wrote it. Her lack of explanation was typical. It probably took every fiber of concentration she possessed just to write that much. I believe she wanted to share this because she could identify herself and her sisters in the story. And it was exciting to see that she also identified herself with the Lord.

Caring for and sharing with Jenny and Ann had been a privilege in spite of many struggles.

A PROMPT ANSWER PLUS BONUS!

Though only a short time in our care, it was long enough to sow a few seeds, create a new awareness, instill a little more love—all for Jesus. Now it seemed like He was allowing us to remain a small part of their lives.

More exciting than the letters was our first phone call, which followed a month later. The long-distance call was further evidence of their mother's willingness to continue our relationship.

"Mark, there's the phone," Earl said with a basket of laundry in his hands. "Here's the keys to the house. I guess you can get it quicker than I can."

Mark ran up from behind, grabbing his dad's keys. We had just returned from the farm and were carrying dirty laundry, leftover food, and fishing gear to the house.

Mark was laughing over the phone as we walked in. Casey concluded it had to be a girl.

"Is it Laurie?" he whispered to Mark as he set down his bag of groceries. Mark shook his head.

"Denise?"

Another negative response.

"Just a minute," Mark said as he cupped his hand over the phone. "Here, Casey, it's someone you know." Casey took the phone from Mark.

"Who is it, Mark?" I asked.

"It's Patti, Jenny and Ann's oldest sister," he responded casually. Patti had lived at the children's home the same time Casey did.

"Patti?" Earl responded. "Why is she calling?"

"Because Jenny and Ann wanted to talk to us," Mark answered.

"Jenny and Ann?" I said surprised. "On the phone? Right now? They called to talk to us?"

"Someone wants you, Pat," Casey said as he handed me the phone.

"Hi, it's me!" a small voice cried. Our connection was unbelievably poor. Though calls to my sister 2,500 miles away sound like she is next door, this one from a distance of forty-five miles sounded like an overseas call.

"Annie-poo, how are you?" I asked excitedly.

"Oh, I wish you wouldn't call me that," she said, annoyed. "You know I don't like it." I laughed. Ann hadn't changed a bit. And I'm sure she felt the same about me and my teasing.

The phone bill must have been astronomical. All five girls wanted to talk with all five of us—individually. How wonderful to be reassured that they were happy and well! The girls were so close to each other. I knew their closeness had helped them a great deal during the separation from their mother.

The girls phoned us about once a month after that. Christmas was fast approaching. We planned to mail our Christmas gifts to them. But, typically, I neglected to get the packages to the post office in time for Christmas arrival. In the middle of January, the gaily decorated packages served as a constant reminder of a neglected deed. Tired of sweeping around the packages, I sat down one day to jot a quick line to the girls' mother.

Would she mind our visiting the girls to give them their Christmas gifts? Not really knowing what to expect, I thought it was worth a try. Seeing the girls after seven months would be great. But I knew the meeting could make both of us uncomfortable.

A phone call only two days later confirmed Anna Jennings's receptiveness to a visit. The following Sunday we gathered together the gifts and started to get ready when the phone rang.

"Pat," Earl called me a few minutes later. "The shift supervisor at the plant just called. I've got to get out there right away. McHaley marked off and Peterson is sick."

"But we can't cancel seeing the girls now," I said, disappointed. "We're supposed to be there in fifteen minutes."

"You and the boys go ahead," he said. "I'm sure they'll understand."

The thought of walking alone into a potentially uncomfortable situation would have bothered me at one time. But with a renewed awareness in Christ came a new boldness and confidence I continue to experience to this day. Knowing the Lord was by my side put the meeting in its proper perspective. And, too, Mrs. Jennings likely was more apprehensive than I.

Mark, Matt, Casey, and I piled into the van—

following Mrs. Jennings's directions exactly.

"OK, guys. Look for a white farmhouse on the right with a red mailbox," I instructed my navigators after we turned on their road.

"This might be it, mom," Matt said. "Slow down."

As we came closer, the boys spotted the red mailbox perched inconspicuously alongside a huge, gnarled, old oak tree. A thin layer of snow covered the ground. A couple of rusted cars stood by an old shed. Two dogs barked warningly.

"For a place with seven people in it, I sure don't see any signs of life," Casey observed as he got out of the van.

"We'll soon find out," I replied.

A handwritten sign in a door on a side porch instructed us to go to the other side of the house. We tracked through the snow according to the instructions. At the end of another porch, a door opened wide to reveal a dark-haired man with a smile on his face.

"Come on in," he greeted us cordially. "We've been wondering where you were. Did you have trouble finding the house? Didn't your husband come?"

Any fears I may have had vanished with the hospitable welcome given us by Tom Jennings. One by one the girls appeared to greet us—very shyly at first. It felt so good to hug them once again. Conspicuously missing was their mother, Anna.

"Come on, mom, we want you to meet them," I heard Jenny whisper coaxingly to her mom, who was in a nearby bedroom. A couple of minutes later Jenny and Ann led her into the kitchen.

"I'm very pleased to meet you," she said shyly. I knew from Jenny's birth certificate that Anna was thirty years old. Her long, dark hair was pulled back tightly into a ponytail. She was dressed neatly in a light purple polyester pantsuit. I had the feeling it was her best outfit. Her smile was Jenny all over. I liked her immediately. She was not at all the ogre I had pictured in my mind.

Tom proudly led a tour through his rented farmhouse—the home he and Anna had worked so hard to renovate for the girls. The house was at its Sunday best. As Anna became acquainted with us, she relaxed in the knowledge that we too were not the image she had pictured.

Tom, Anna, and I sat in the living room. After a time, we felt free to discuss that period when the girls had been in foster care.

"News travels fast in small towns, and I found out where Patti and Brenda were staying," she told me. Patti and Brenda's foster home at the Millers was in a rural setting not too many miles from their mother.

"We'd drive by just so Anna could see the girls playing in the yard," Tom added. "I didn't like to do that, because it always made her cry.

"We were trying our best to save enough money

for a down payment on a house so we could get the girls back. I'm still working the two jobs I worked then. But either I'd get sick or she'd get sick, and we'd have doctor bills and never could seem to get caught up."

Anna pulled out a tissue to blot away the tears that welled in her eyes. "The girls told me to keep praying, to have faith in the Lord," she said. "I thought if they had so much faith, maybe I should too. Finally, we found this house. The landlord gave it to us rent-free during the time we cleaned and repaired it."

Tom had earlier pointed out his handiwork as he showed us through the old farmhouse. He had installed a new furnace with duct work, paneled several walls, painted, patched, and reinforced.

Talking with Tom and Anna added for me another dimension to the foster-care picture—that of the natural parents. Anna never had much in a material sense. She married young and didn't finish school. A series of pregnancies, which included the births of her girls, two stillborns, and a number of miscarriages in between, left her physically exhausted. Trying to cope with five small children and a husband who drank and worked only half the time left her mentally exhausted as well.

The only answer appeared to be foster care while she sought a divorce. Soon after, she married Tom. Through him she was able to pull her fragmented life back together. But it didn't happen overnight. It had taken a number of years before she reached a breaking point. Picking up the pieces took even longer.

The Lord's directing hand surely was with this woman. All her children had been placed in Christian homes. Her second marriage was to a man reared in the southern Baptist traditions. Tom had been trained in the ways of the Lord. Proverbs 22:6 gave me hope that he would assume the responsibility of seeking religious training for the girls.

The family, he told me, was actively looking for church membership. At that point, their selection was narrowed to two or three Christian parishes.

"We've overstayed our welcome," I said, not really wanting to leave.

"Not at all," Tom replied. "We know how you feel about the girls, and they're always talking about you. Come out anytime you want to see them. We appreciate what you've done for them. You're always welcome."

On our way home, parts of our conversation came back to me. Anna had experienced a living hell I couldn't begin to relate to. Tears came to my eyes, knowing how wrong I had been to prejudge her.

Of course, we had seen the home and family at its best. Financial problems would continue to plague Tom. Caring for a family of seven would always be a burden for Anna. Making do with second best probably will always be their way of life. Though in many ways their home compared unfavorably with ours and their hardships seemed so much more insurmountable than ours, here is where the girls naturally belonged. Their roots, their very identity, was with their mother, who loved and wanted them.

Seeing the love and happiness resulting from the Lord's guiding hand in this family's lives was exhilarating. Through Him a primary aim of the foster care system—to preserve and strengthen the child's natural home—had been accomplished.

Unfortunately, theirs is a rare case of success.

Being confident of this very thing, that he which hath begun a good work in you will perform it until the day of Jesus Christ. (Phil. 1:6) chapter thirteen

Casey's New Home

"I don't want to alarm you, Pat, but Casey has had an accident." It was Sister Mary Ann calling from the hospital.

"What happened?" I asked, astounded. Only forty-five minutes ago he and I had eaten dinner together. I had just finished the dishes. After asking permission, he had left to ride around the neighborhood on Matt's bike.

"Casey was hit by a car," she answered. "He rode his bike against a red light. He was knocked to the hood of the car, which probably saved him from more extensive injuries."

Casey now was in the emergency room with a broken leg. At this point he had lived with us only a few days. In the confusion of the accident, he couldn't remember our last name and had given the ambulance attendants Sister Mary Ann's name to contact.

I felt so badly for him. He hadn't even had time to adjust to his new home. So much emotional turmoil this young boy had gone through, and now this.

"I'll be right over," I told Sister.

"Good," she replied. "I'll be leaving here shortly. But call me at the children's home if you need anything. I'll notify Mrs. Crawford. I'm sure she'll be contacting you."

Earl and the boys had left only a day earlier for a fishing trip to Canada with grandpa. (Recuperated from his accident by this time, grandpa had moved back into his own home.) Casey and I stayed behind, not wanting to intrude on a vacation designed especially for grandpa in an effort to help balance what so far had been a difficult year for him.

The route to the hospital was all too familiar. Grandma Bilow had been there five weeks before she died, Grandpa Bilow for two weeks after his accident, and now Casey—all within a four-month period.

After I arrived, a nurse directed me to Casey's room. He was crying softly when I entered.

"Do you have a lot of pain, Casey?" I asked.

"I just want my mom," he answered, turning his head away from me. A fresh trickle of tears cascaded down his face. I took his hand.

"Casey, I'm sorry your mom can't be here with you now. I really am. After Mrs. Crawford tells her about your accident, I'm sure she'll be up to visit you." He brightened a bit at that thought. The doctors had told him he would be in for several days.

Casey basked in the attention he received

CASEY'S NEW HOME

during the next few weeks. While visiting him in the hospital and during his recuperation at home I met a lot of his friends from the children's home—volunteer helpers, house parents, staff workers—all of whom spoke highly of him. Many who also knew the girls pulled me aside.

"A home like yours is just what Casey needs," his former house parent told me. "He's really pleased about it, and so are we."

Casey obviously enjoyed all the visits. But the two people he most wanted to see—his parents—never came.

He soon returned home, dressed in a full leg cast complete with graffiti and crutches. The cast, to be worn eight weeks, didn't quite make it. A portion had to be reinforced—thanks to some well-intentioned efforts.

"Hey, Case, that cast is filthy," Mark told him one day while they listened to the stereo in their bedroom.

"Yeah, I know," he replied. "Where is that list of instructions I brought home from the hospital? It tells how to clean it." The two searched diligently through their belongings until they found the dogeared sheet.

"Shoe polish," Casey said. "It says you can clean it with shoe polish. Do we have any?"

"I think there's some downstairs," Mark replied. "I'll do it for you, Casey. We'll make it good as new." Mark rushed downstairs to find the white shoe polish. He was anxious to tackle the "cast painting."

They spent the next hour using a whole bottle of polish on the fingerprinted, dirt-stained cast. The finished product looked beautiful. The graffiti was preserved. But the cast, unfortunately, was not. The liquid shoe polish quickly softened the plaster, which cracked through a brightly painted, red Cupid's heart right down the middle.

There was one very upset intern when we returned to the hospital several days later for a plaster reinforcement.

Casey adjusted quickly to his new surroundings. While Mark attended a parochial high school, Casey went to a public high school. We felt separate schools would give the boys time away from each other. Each could establish his own identity in his own school without feeling threatened by the other.

We hoped that a new family environment would provide Casey with motivation to improve his school work. His last grade card indicated he had given up. Written comments by his teachers included, "Casey seems to try to get by with as little work as possible" and, "Casey just doesn't work!"

Art was his favorite subject and one in which he did exceptionally well. So Earl and I encouraged him to pursue that field. His musical abilities included compositions of his own, which further substantiated his creative ability.

It was a red-letter day when first-quarter grades indicated his renewed interest in school.

"Pat, I got my grade card today," he announced proudly as he came bounding up the stairs to my office.

"Great, Casey! Where is it?" I asked.

"Here, take a look." With a grin on his face, he handed me the card.

"Not bad, Casey, not bad!" I responded. He received an *A* in art, with average grades in his other subjects. Casey had warned me earlier about his math grade, which he promised to work harder at.

"What kinds of projects have you completed in art that you were able to do so well?" I asked.

Casey pulled from a folder some of his latest artwork. Proudly he showed lettering with India ink on plastic sheets and box-type drawings shaded for depth. The work obviously displayed talent.

"This is great, Casey," I told him. "You really should take as many art courses as you can."

"I'm going to, Pat," he answered. "Next year I want to take lettering and graphic printmaking."

As he turned to go change his clothes, he added, "Today Mark and I should clean our bedroom, right?"

"Yes, I guess it is Thursday, isn't it."

Casey came home from school an hour earlier

than Mark. Nine times out of ten, each Thursday he would have the bedroom completely cleaned before Mark came home. Today, however, was the exception. It dawned on me after a while that I didn't hear the usual noises associated with cleaning. Giving in to a creative urge, he had shelved the cleaning to draw a picture of Snoopy for the family bulletin board.

Lest I make Casey look like an angel, let me assure you he was not. Foster kids quickly learn how to impress people. They can become very adept at sizing up an individual and manipulating him to get what they want.

So often, I believe, well-intentioned service groups (and individuals too) try to buy the love of kids who live in institutions by paying their admission fees into movies and amusement parks and by buying them candy and ice cream. The kids know this and play it to the hilt. They take as much as the group or individual will give, but gain only a temporary satisfaction that leaves them with an even bigger appetite for more. Rather, I believe the children need a giving from the heart. A little piece of a person to know that someone really cares. Because children in institutions and foster homes come into a place with a deep sense of rejection, they carry a greater need than most other children for attention and affection. When this need is not met, they develop an insatiable appetite for it.

According to Dr. Edward Zigler in his keynote speech delivered at the First National Conference of Foster Parents held in 1971 in Chicago, with little emotional or intellectual energy to spare for other pursuits, foster children may seem perverse or stupid even though they have good potential for intelligent, constructive learning and behavior.

Dr. Zigler also pointed out that many foster children come into placement wary of adults. The foster child may have a fear that the foster parents are much the same as other adults who have perhaps punished him or denied him love and affection. This, he added, makes it doubly important to balance criticism with heavy doses of love and praise to help the child regain a positive self-image.

Although I didn't see this at the time, perhaps that was the reason for Casey's wariness toward Earl. He once told me he hated his father. Casey, a real dog lover, told us his father intentionally killed his puppy. By the time he came into institutional care, Casey had suffered innumerable hurts and indiscretions. Noticeably so, he had a difficult time relating to Earl.

There was one man, however, who did win Casey's trust and confidence. That was Jack Cable, a member of Big Brothers, a nonprofit organization that teams responsible men with fatherless boys for one-to-one relationships. Jack and Casey were a Big Brother match.

Casey was pleased the day Jack came to visit him, shortly after he returned from the hospital. And Jack was pleased with the surprise birthday cake we made for him.

"This is great," he told us as he downed another bite of the angel food cake. "But thirty-two candles are a bit much to blow out!" He and Casey laughed. Obviously, the two had built a fine relationship.

Jack made it clear to Casey that he was available any time Casey needed him. But he stopped initiating contact so that Casey and Earl could build a father/son relationship. Still, Casey continued to confide in Jack rather than Earl.

Though I don't know where Casey stands today in his Christian walk, it is very gratifying to know he once did accept Christ. A Young Life camp weekend he and Mark attended so inspired him that he made a stand for the Lord.

Later I would learn his faith in the Lord had taken root much earlier in his life. Diary entries found after he ran away from home revealed how he was trying to trust in the Lord while living at the children's home. "We went to chapel today. I really want to have faith and trust in God. I'm learning to depend on Him."

Other entries depicted how he longed to have his family reunited. He recorded many feelings of disappointment when his mother didn't show up for scheduled visits.

CASEY'S NEW HOME

After the Young Life weekend, Casey came to realize that his body was the temple of the Holy Spirit. He confided in Mark his desire to give up cigarettes. And, for a while at least, he did.

Mark and Casey experimented with cigarettes about the same time. Who influenced whom is still a mystery to us. I actually believe both gave in to their own separate peer pressure groups at school. Another incident in which we still don't know the instigator involved Mark and Casey stealing Christmas tree lights from a neighbor's outside fir tree. Casey, however, was the first to apologize and return the bulbs to the neighbor, with Mark reluctantly following.

Later, Casey's running away would induce Mark to test his own independence. Earl and I would repeat once again, this time concerning our own son, the torment we previously went through three different times with Casey.

But to remember Casey is not simply to think of the trouble he caused. Given the same set of circumstances in the same timing, who among us can cast the first stone?

Rather, to remember Casey is to remember him in his new home. A renewed interest in school, a crazy straw fight at the farm, sleeping in the wheat field under the stars, making brownies or fudge together and licking the pan clean, playing guitars, and forever popping corn.

But most important of all, to remember Casey

is to visualize a confused boy checking out Christianity from the sidelines . . . and then making a commitment.

> My sheep hear my voice, and I know them, and they follow me: And I give unto them eternal life; and they shall never perish, neither shall any man pluck them out of my hand. (John 10:27-28)

chapter fourteen
Casey Rebels

Matt picked up the phone again. It was still busy.

"Mom, Casey's been on the phone ever since he got home from school," he complained. "Now he's talking to his brother."

I winced a bit, wondering how to handle this. The long-distance toll call wasn't stopping the two from making more frequent contact. I had been told Casey's brother had been a negative influence on him. The older boy drifted from one set of problems into another. Mrs. Crawford advised us to try to keep contact to a minimum.

I mouthed a "Matt wants to use the phone" to Casey and then went to my office to work an hour or two. It wasn't long afterward that he came up to talk.

"That was my brother," he said. "My grandpa died yesterday. Can you take me to the funeral?" He seemed almost pleased, not that his grandfather had died, but because this incident was his—apart from us. It involved *his* family.

"When is it, Casey?" I asked.

"I don't know yet," he answered. "My brother is

going to call back."

"I'll talk to Mrs. Crawford about it, and we'll see what we can do," I promised him. "I'm sorry, Casey, about your grandpa. Were you close to him?"

"He took me fishing sometimes," he answered. "We had a lot of fun together." He didn't volunteer any more information. The subject was dropped.

Casey's rather calm reaction to his grandfather's death led me to believe he would take this, too, in stride. Perhaps the reality of the death had not set in, or he simply concealed his emotions (as he so often did). But we would soon discover just how deeply he did grieve.

Mrs. Crawford called a day or two later to tell us that the funeral was scheduled the following day in a town sixty miles away. Because the funeral was on a Saturday, the agency had no driver for transporting. Earl was scheduled for overtime work that day.

"I don't think Casey saw his grandfather very often," Mrs. Crawford said. "And I'm not so sure that it's a good idea for him to see his older brother right now." Casey's brother John had called him long-distance several times during the past month. John wanted Casey to move in with him and their father, who was living with a woman. The three of them and the woman's two small children lived in a mobile home.

I recalled one of the nuns at the children's home once warning me about the negative influence John had on Casey. John drifted from one problem into another, she said. Stealing was a problem for both the boys in their earlier days at the home. And I knew since then John had gone through several drug programs.

I also remembered Casey bitterly saying he hated his father for killing his puppy and Casey's seeming indifference to his grandfather's death.

"I don't think at this particular time it's to Casey's best interests to attend that funeral," Mrs. Crawford said upon reflection.

"I think you're right," I agreed.

We would soon find our judgment to be completely wrong.

The director of an education and research center on death at the University of Minnesota once said, "It's important not to assume, because a child is mute and seemingly indifferent to loss, that he doesn't have profound feelings. Children react very profoundly to death. Like a young rabbit in danger, they freeze. It's very important to address that numbing."

Had Casey attended the funeral, perhaps he would have had the opportunity to act out his grief with his family whom he loved.

About a month prior to this time, Casey formed a friendship with Craig, another troubled fourteen-year-old. Craig's parents also were divorced. His father, whom he disliked intensely, had legal custody of him and his brother. Over the past two years, Craig had run away from home nearly a dozen times. Punishments inflicted upon Craig by his father for running away only intensified Craig's dislike for him. Several times he was ordered to get severely short haircuts.

The relationship I hoped would build between Earl and Casey never really materialized. Perhaps he associated Earl with his father. And, too, Earl could not tolerate deceitfulness. Try as I might, I could not make Earl look at some of the underlying reasons for Casey's behavior. The more I tried to help Casey, the more alienated Earl felt.

I believe it takes a very special set of people with an extremely strong marriage and deep-rooted faith to withstand the pressures that can be imposed by a troubled teenager. Couples (and individuals too) contemplating foster care for this age group should be made aware of and trained to cope with the even more complex situations that can and often do arise during the care of a foster teenager.

These problems for us surfaced the day I found this note in my typewriter:

Dear Pat,
I am leaving for a while and do not get worried about me. I want to get away from my problems. I don't like it when you always ask me a question like what's the matter or something like that. What I am saying is that

I want to be alone. I think the reason I was like that today is because my grandpa died. I probably won't get to see my family for a while because I'm doing this. Well not much time, got to go.

Casey

P.S. I will be all right. Please just leave me alone for a while. (AND DON'T WORRY)

"He's just cooling off," Earl said.

"But what's he cooling off about?" I asked. There had been no arguments, no differences of opinion. Only a sullen moodiness which I tried to get him to talk about. How I wished at times that he would show physical signs of anger. Instead he silently seethed inside with resentment and frustration—building up to a point of explosion.

"He'll come back," Earl reassured me. "Just give him time."

The hours and minutes slowly ticked by. Casey didn't show up for dinner. The four of us ate in silence.

By nine that evening we called the police. Earl and I had exhausted all possibilities. The neighbors were aware of his disappearance. We had combed the area by car to no avail. Mrs. Crawford had been informed and now the police. All we could do was wait.

During the weeks ahead we learned a valuable lesson about runaways. Our fear for Casey's welfare drove us all over the city in search of him. There are a zillion nooks and crannies in any given city in which a teenage runaway can hide. Searching is futile. And when a runaway knows you are pursuing him, he runs even faster and farther. Waiting until the child returns of his own volition is just about a parent's only alternative.

"In quietness and in confidence shall be your strength" (Isa. 30:15). If Earl and I (myself in particular) would have followed this comforting piece of Scripture, how much emotionally draining energy would we have saved? Prayerfully waiting and trusting in the Lord could have been a recharging experience. Instead we chose to spin our wheels in frustration looking for Casey.

About midnight the phone rang. It was one of our neighbors. Casey had sought refuge with their daughter. Tremendously relieved, I shot up a prayer of thanksgiving. He was soon back home. But not for long.

A recent article appearing in *The Blade* (Toledo's daily newspaper) states, "A half million children, nearly four times as many as in 1961, now live with foster parents in the United States. More than 50 percent are taken from parents with emotional or drinking problems, an amazing 31 percent have parents who simply don't want them, 3.1 percent are orphans and fewer than 2 percent are handicapped or retarded." It would be interesting to know how many of those 500,000 children have been in foster care for more than two years.

I believe Casey (as countless others) is a classic example of a foster child who has been left hanging far too long in limbo. And this isn't necessarily the fault of our caseworkers and social service agencies. A large part of the problem seems to lie within our judicial system.

Robert and Dorothy DeBolt, adoptive parents of twenty children (most of whom are handicapped) and subjects of a book entitled *Nineteen Steps Up the Mountain*, recently appeared in our city for a speaking engagement. Said Mrs. DeBolt, "The slightest degree of parenting seems to be justification to keep foster kids in limbo forever. Parents who visit their kids on Christmas and Easter think they are doing their job as parents."

The juvenile court judge of whom I spoke earlier says, "Every single case I have on termination of rights goes up on appeal no matter what is in the record. And courts of appeals will refuse to terminate parental rights if there is the slightest interest at all on the part of the parents that they want their kids."

The court process, of course, is a lengthy one. A short year for an adult can be an extremely long one for a child. One example of lengthy foster care cited by the judge involves a child who was taken from his parents at the age of five. By the time the child was ten, parental rights were terminated. The case was taken to the Court of

Appeals, where it sat for a year before it was discovered that a portion of the trial record was missing. The judge had to retry a phase of the initial trial for the record. The case will go up on appeal again. Meanwhile, the child, who was taken from his parents at age five, now is twelve and one-half. While shorter periods of foster care are becoming more common, many, many children still become lost in the system.

Another problem appears to be our caseworkers' lack of training in judicial procedures. "Attorneys make mincemeat out of us," says one social worker. "They have a way of making us feel like we are on trial rather than the natural parents."

To ease this problem, our local court, in conjunction with the county social service agency for children, now offers periodic seminars to educate caseworkers on the workings of the court. Mock trials are set up so that caseworkers can be trained to know how to collect and document evidence. Foster parents are asked to keep daily records on the foster child. (How I lament the fact I never did this. Today, the written accounts would have been invaluable.)

After four years of living in an in-limbo state, is it any wonder Casey rebelled? His nervousness and anxiety continued to accelerate. By this time Casey's friend Craig, who was in a similar state, joined forces with him. The two affirmed each other. Together they defied authority by skipping school, lying, and stealing.

Twice more Casey would run away from home. After the second time, Earl refused to have any more to do with him. I continued to hold on, which I can see in retrospect as a mistake. We could do no more for Casey. He no longer wanted to live with us. And he would try everything in his power to make us not want him. But I didn't recognize the need to let go. God did use us for a period of growth in Casey's life. But now he needed more than we could give. It was past time for him to move on to someone else whom the Lord would provide to fill his needs.

Earlier that day my brother Tom came to visit.

"What's the matter, Pat?" he said cheerily. "You look like the last rose of summer."

I smiled, surprised that my face showed that much expression. The Lord knew I needed a lift just at that moment. Tom's cheerfulness was just enough to pull me out of the pits for a while.

"It's Casey, Tom," I answered. "He's run away again, and Earl said he won't take him back."

Tom always enjoyed Casey and had been a Big Brother once himself. He listened carefully to the events leading up to the second running away.

"The school called to tell us Casey hadn't attended classes," I told him. "After the last time he ran away, Casey promised he wouldn't skip any more school.

"When he and Craig came home at the usual

time, I asked them how school was. Casey's response was, 'Great, but I've got a lot of catching up to do.' I told him the school had called us to let us know of his absence. He knew he was caught, and I literally exploded with anger."

The past month had been trying for us. Earl was working a lot of double and even some triple (twenty-four-hour) shifts. After undergoing his second surgery for an arthritic knee, he was experiencing an increasing amount of pain. His job, which required an unusual amount of walking, was becoming steadily more difficult for him to perform. The burden of Casey's unwanted behavior was left for me to cope with a good portion of the time. And Casey knew exactly how to handle me to get what he wanted.

I told Tom how Earl and I sat with the boys in the living room, trying to uncover their reason for cutting classes. We thought it was strange when Craig followed Casey into the dining room and the two whispered a few brief words to each other. Earl called them back into the living room. Within a matter of minutes the two signaled each other. Craig ran out the front door while Casey tore for the back, grabbing a jacket on his way out.

"Pat, I'd like to help," Tom offered. "If Elaine consents and we clear it with your social worker, maybe Casey might like to live with us. We have an extra bedroom now that Billy moved out."

Billy was Tom's eighteen-year-old stepson, who

recently left home to be on his own. Casey had always liked Tom and Elaine and their two small children. This would be an entirely different situation for him. He loved little children. Tom's kids would not be his rivals as perhaps Mark and Matt were. And, too, Tom had experience with teenage boys through Billy and his association with Big Brothers.

Tom's offer was like an answer to prayer. But what seemed a provision by God for Casey actually would turn out to be a provision for us.

At three the next morning the phone rang. It was Craig's dad. The boys were picked up by the police while riding a stolen motorcycle. If no one came to get them, they would be sent to the juvenile detention center for further disposition. Did Earl want to ride along with him to get Casey? He stubbornly refused. But he didn't try to stop me from going, although I could sense it was his will that I stay home.

If I would have heeded Ephesians 5:22 ("Wives, submit yourselves unto your own husbands, as unto the Lord"), the vandalism and subsequent anguish of the next several months would have been prevented. Casey and Craig likely would not have the juvenile records they now have. And the two would have been physically separated—the best treatment under the circumstances for both.

The trip to pick up the boys was emotionally upsetting, to say the least. Craig's father clearly was at a loss as to how to deal with his son. The strict discipline he received as a boy hadn't worked with Craig.

The inky black night seemed just the right setting to complement the traumatic circumstances. We entered a large old building and walked down a long corridor toward a switchboard operator who manned an outdated switchboard. The board was silent now. Its only use for the moment was to hold a steaming hot cup of coffee.

An intake worker dressed in blue jeans came out to escort us into a large room. Friendly but direct, she explained how the boys were picked up.

"About two this morning two policemen spotted the boys traveling down Cherry Street," she explained. "Strangely enough, they weren't picked up for stealing the motorcycle, but because they looked so young. The police knew they were runaways. They treated them to some hamburgers and French fries and then brought them here."

Before seeing the boys, we had to answer several questions. I explained to her about Tom's desire to obtain a foster care license in order to provide a home for Casey. After calling Tom to confirm his offer, I promised the worker I'd call Mrs. Crawford first thing in the morning.

With that I was taken to a different room. While waiting for Casey I heard Craig in tears scream at his dad that he didn't want to go home—that he hated him.

I closed my eyes in despair. Hearing a son say that to his father made me tremble. Dear Lord, how do lives get so horribly messed up?

At that moment Casey walked in. I was startled. The look in his eyes was one of pure hatred. Still trembling and now teary-eyed, I walked over and hugged him tightly.

"Casey, don't look at me like that. I love you very much. Don't you know that?" The strange look of hatred and defiance melted into the old familiar Casey grin. We looked at each other and laughed. The tension of the moment slipped into a peace-filled relief. After we sat down to wait for Craig and his dad, Casey began to talk.

"I was really glad when the police picked us up. We were tired and hungry. We didn't have any money, and we didn't know where we were going to sleep."

"Casey, obviously you don't want to live with us anymore," I said.

"I really want to live with my mom or my dad," he said despairingly. "Can't you talk to Mrs. Crawford about that?"

I understood from several different sources that his mother had long promised her children to move into a home so they could be reunited. The house she finally moved into turned out to be a two-bedroom apartment that was shared with her mother. I also understood she was pregnant. That situation looked hopeless as did his father's. He was living in a trailer with a woman who had two small children. Casey's brother also lived with them.

I promised Casey I would ask Mrs. Crawford to talk with him.

"In the meantime, how would you feel about living with Tom and Elaine?" I asked. His eyes brightened a little.

"With Paul and Brenda?" (Those were Tom and Elaine's children.)

"Yes," I answered. "With Paul and Brenda."

"I think I'd like that," he said.

"But no more contact with Craig," I warned.

"OK," he said. "I won't."

Our situation seemed, temporarily at least, smoothed over. But Craig reacted like he didn't want to go home. Both boys were dirty, with windblown hair that was knotted into ringlets of curls. With head bowed, and a tear-stained face, Craig looked like a whipped puppy.

My heart went out to both him and his dad. Neither could understand the feelings nor the actions of the other. They were making each other's lives a living hell and didn't know how to stop. (Our Young Life Bible study group continues periodically to pray for Craig and his dad.)

Casey and I stopped home long enough for him to shower and pack a few things. By five-thirty that morning he was in his new home. This one would last five days.

> Let us therefore come boldly unto the throne of grace, that we may obtain mercy, and find grace to help in time of need. (Heb. 4:16)

chapter fifteen

"And I Feel the World Is Coming to an End"

Casey's removal from our home was a relief. Though Tom's house was a short distance from ours, Casey came over only to pick up clothes and belongings as he needed them. During his short visits, I sensed that he, too, was relieved to find a new home. We all began to breathe a little easier.

While sorting through some of Casey's possessions a day or two later, I picked up a sheet of paper that fell out of a school notebook. As I began sliding it back, the title caught my eye. It was a song Casey wrote in memory of his grandfather. Like the force of a magnet, one word drew me to the next:

"My Grandpa"
by Casey Martin

My grandpa died on March 9, 1978,
And in my heart that isn't so great.
Life has to end one day or another,
He was as close to me as my sister and my brother.

And I feel the world is coming to an end,
And the world is coming to an end,
And I don't have no one to send,
Because the world is coming to an end.
I think.

My grandpa use to take me on his bicycle,
And one thing that I really loved was sour
   pickles.
We use to have good times when we were out
   there,
But now he is gone and I don't know where.
And I feel the world is coming to an end,
And the world is coming to an end,
And I don't have no one to send,
Because I think the world is coming to an end.

How hopeless the world must have seemed to Casey! "And the world is coming to an end, And I don't have no one to send." If only he could have felt the comforting reassurance that hope was his—that someone had been sent. The price was paid! Praise God when the world does come to an end for those who have faith. "Believe on the Lord Jesus Christ, and thou shalt be saved" (Acts 16:31).

I reread the song several times more and noticed something else. The words "I think" and "I feel" stood out like a small ray of light penetrating ever so slightly through the negativism of Casey's

"AND I FEEL THE WORLD IS COMING TO AN END"

words. He had once made a commitment to Christ. Through those words did he recognize the hope that can be found in Jesus Christ—hope in a world teeming with dead-end roads?

I made copies of the song and a forged note I found excusing Casey from school. Perhaps Mrs. Crawford could seek counseling to help Casey overcome this depression. But by the time she received the copies, it was too late. He was gone. Tom came over to explain what happened.

"I knew Casey and Craig were keeping in touch by phone," he said. "But Casey seemed to enjoy being with us. He was great about keeping the few rules we did impose. I couldn't believe it when he called me to say he'd be five minutes late last night. Just couldn't believe it! Billy never did that. And Casey was great with the kids!"

Tom shook his head, unable to figure out why Casey had left.

"Up to this point, I refused to let Craig come over," he continued. "But when the two of them said they wanted to go to a youth group meeting at Craig's synagogue, I thought this might be the best thing for them."

I recalled Craig's father telling me how active Craig had been at one time in this group. He even attended a regional conference with them. Mrs. Crawford once told us that Casey, when living with his family, was the only one of his brothers and sisters who attended a weekly Christian club for children.

"They left right after dinner," Tom added. It was now nearly midnight. Once again we called the police and informed Mrs. Crawford. All we could do now was pray for the Lord's protection.

Meanwhile, Casey and Craig were letting air out of tires and breaking into the synagogue's gift shop. Their booty—a grocery bag full of bubble gum and assorted pieces of jewelry, which included both expensive pieces and small trinkets—was left behind at our house after Matt's surprise visit during the vandalism the next day.

A detective later uncovered their theft of a puppy from a nearby pet store. When asked the reason, Casey replied, "Raisin was the Bilows' dog, not mine. I wanted one of my own." (The puppy never was found.)

Marcia T. Gedanken, a social service consultant at the time she wrote an article published by the Child Welfare League of America, Inc. (*On Fostering: Fifteen Articles by and for Foster Parents*), outlined a number of problems associated with foster parents. We were guilty of Problem Number Two—the deep lack of understanding of how children feel about foster family placement. She states, "Foster parents are particularly insensitive to the insecure and awkward position of a child who is not in his own family. They insist that because they treat the child as their own, the child feels like their own. Most foster children do not, and cannot, even when a positive, inner identification takes place."

How true that is! And the sooner foster parents recognize this, the better. Our understanding of this came too late.

Casey and Craig were gone all night. The next day Earl and I went to work as usual. (Here, too, I can see the Lord's hand at work. I found a part-time job in our community as a public relations writer for a social service agency which serves as an umbrella agency over scores of others in a four-county area. The two-day-a-week position left me time to free-lance at home. While my past days in the corporate world revolved around dollars and profits, this job centered on services and people. It was an entirely different field, and I loved it!)

It was Holy Week—Maundy Thursday. After spending the night at the student union of our local university, Casey and Craig were tired and hungry. Casey knew I would be working that day. And he still had a key to our house. They could eat without fear of being apprehended.

We later learned from the detective who questioned both boys what happened that morning. Both were punchy after being up most of the night. Neither was on drugs, according to the detective. They may have been drinking, as evidenced by a half-filled can of beer found on the television set.

While eating, one boy spilled his milk which,

in turn, tipped over the salt shaker. Both thought that was funny. Messing up the kitchen a bit might be fun. (And I understand this was Casey's idea.) They knew they were already in trouble. So what was a little more?

The boys admitted to getting carried away. Casey's hurt and frustration finally surfaced after all those years as they escalated their acts of vandalism and destruction.

He seemed to single me out in his violence. He knew what would hurt the most. My new steel-string guitar and its fur-lined case were hideously sprayed with red paint. Added to that were dripping raw eggs. How many times had we played guitar together?

He knew how each day I looked forward to the mail. Every piece was torn, including a devotional booklet with several newly published devotions I had written. Oddly enough, one was about Casey and his broken leg, along with his picture.

All our winter coats were thrown on the floor. Only mine was spray painted. In our bedroom every compartment of my jewelry box was filled with a conglomeration of shampoos, aftershaves, and liquid medications absconded from the medicine cabinet. Earl's jewelry box remained untouched. Casey never hated or even disliked me. Was he seeking revenge with his own mother?

Later, when my mother came over, all I could do was hug her and cry. How little I appreciated her

"AND I FEEL THE WORLD IS COMING TO AN END"

sometimes!

Sleep that night in the motel room was nearly impossible. Earl tossed and turned, finally resorting to tranquilizers. The emotional pressure during the next several months, coupled with the arthritic pain of his knee, would drive him to depend more than he should on medications.

The traffic through the house for the next several days (and weeks) was unbelievable. Neighbors toured the house in shock and bolted their own doors in fear. Friends, relatives, insurance people, friends of friends, agency caseworkers, Young Life kids, detectives, workers—all viewed the disaster. Some out of curiosity and disbelief. Others as part of their jobs.

The first day after the vandalism was lost to a mass of telephone calls and visits involving insurance, police, and cleaning details. I couldn't recall a more depressing Good Friday. The suffering and humiliation Jesus underwent that day nearly two thousand years ago somehow meant more now. I truly recognized for the first time how worldly possessions can be removed in an instant, as can someone whom you love. Eventually, all those whom we love of this world will fail us at one time or another. "But the Lord shall endure for ever" (Ps. 9:7).

Saturday morning we left the motel early to take an inventory of the damage for the insurance company. Each morning entering the house was like enduring another shock. We knew what to expect, but yet, viewing the shambles after a twelve-hour break seemed always to uncover more atrocities not yet discovered.

We labored half a day amid more phone calls and visits. Our neighbor, Jean Montaine, and I had just finished taking the room-by-room inventory when Earl's sister, Janice, came over with her sister-in-law. While talking, we heard someone crying. It was Matt, sitting on the edge of his bed.

"Look at this, dad," he cried. "My bedroom's ruined." He started to sob uncontrollably. "Why . . . d-did he d-do it, mom? I . . . never h-hurt him. I . . . l-liked him." As I watched large tears flow from Matt's beautiful brown eyes, I wondered too. Why?

Matt's breakdown was enough to set off Mark.

"No, Mark, don't do that!" Janice was calling out from Mark's bedroom. Earl and I ran to see what was wrong.

"Why not?" Mark replied angrily. "He deserves a lot worse than this." In a fit of rage Mark sought revenge by applying a half-empty bottle of aftershave to Casey's clothes.

With pain Earl and I looked at each other. In the confusion of the past couple of days, we hadn't thought about Mark and Matt and the effect the vandalism was having on them.

"I'll take the kids home with me," Janice said, taking me aside. "Next week is spring vacation.

"AND I FEEL THE WORLD IS COMING TO AN END"

Let them stay with us the whole week."

"Oh, would you?" I asked in relief.

"This is too much for them," Earl said, he too recognizing their need to get away. "We'll move to the motel nearer your house, and the kids can use the pool."

"I think we need a break, too, Earl," I said later after Janice and the boys left. We decided to stay away from the house on Easter Sunday and relax at the motel. To further remove our minds from the tension of the past few days, the Montaines offered to spend the remainder of the weekend with us at the motel. They registered in the room next to ours. The eight of us enjoyed a leisurely dinner followed later by relaxing conversation at the pool. It was like living in a completely different world for a while.

When we finally returned to our motel room Saturday night, the phone was ringing.

"Hello?" Matt answered. "She's right here. Just a minute, Aunt Elaine."

"Mrs. Crawford called," she told me. "The boys are in custody."

I sank down on the bed in relief. I hadn't realized how worried I was for their safety as well as for ours and our neighbors.

"Oh, Elaine, I can't believe it." What would happen to them now, I wondered.

Casey and Craig had taken Mark and Matt's

bikes for transportation. But evidently they ditched them to hitchhike to Casey's dad's home town sixty miles away. Did Casey think someone in his family would shelter them? Or did he simply want to visit and move on? No one knows. But, undoubtedly, he wasn't prepared for the abrupt end to their four-day rampage. Elaine was told that his one remaining living grandfather turned them over to the police. Later, an authority told us it was his uncle.

Mrs. Crawford told Elaine that the boys would be transferred to the juvenile detention center in our county the next morning. We slept in relief that night.

Church the following morning was crowded. Easter Sunday. The day to celebrate victory through Christ over sin, death, and the power of the devil. "Jesus Christ has risen today, Alleluia!" we sang. I felt renewed. "For in the time of trouble he shall hide me in his pavilion: in the secret of his tabernacle shall he hide me; he shall set me upon a rock" (Ps. 27:5).

Here with others in the body of Christ we sang, loved, praised, and even cried. Here was warmth, love, strength, and affirmation. Here I sat upon the rock.

But Casey was alone—separated from Craig, who must have been like a brother to him by now. Did his faith in Christ help him get through that day?

"AND I FEEL THE WORLD IS COMING TO AN END"

Craig's dad, who went to visit his son, told us what he saw as he walked past Casey's small cubicle, which contained only a small bunk bed. Inside was a defeated fourteen-year-old boy who was dressed in a uniform and a pair of ill-fitting tennis shoes. Sitting on the floor with his back against the wall, he had tears rolling down his face.

The young boy had no visitors that day. No parents, no foster parents, no friends or relatives, no agency people. He was alone. Alone with his thoughts.

> And I feel the world is coming to an end,
> And the world is coming to an end,
> And I don't have no one to send,
> Because I think the world is coming to an end.

> And he said unto me, My grace is sufficient for thee: for my strength is made perfect in weakness. (II Cor. 12:9)

chapter sixteen
A Negative Turns Into Positives

The stench was indescribable. The combination of odors from six dozen rotting eggs along with spoiled food, sweet perfumes, and a variety of liquid items from the medicine cabinet—all left over a four-day period—noxiously filled every corner of the house.

It was nine o'clock Monday morning. The professional cleaners were due at nine-thirty. I walked gingerly through garbage strewn on the kitchen floor into the dining room and gagged.

"Pat, why don't you go to Jean's house until the cleaners get here," Earl suggested softly as he put his arms around my shoulders. The reality of the situation once again hit us after our short absence from home. "I'll just wait on the front steps until they come," he added.

We were both anxious to start getting the house back in order. But standing in the midst of the debris and stench was overwhelming. Where should we start?

"I think I will go to Jean's," I responded to Earl's suggestion. Maybe once the cleaners came, we would both feel more motivated.

Thirty minutes later I was back. The cleaners still had not arrived. Impatient, I called to find the reason for the delay.

"I'm terribly sorry, Mrs. Bilow," the manager said. "The insurance company canceled our services."

"But I don't understand," I responded with disbelief. "Why?"

"It seems there's some question about insurance coverage," he continued. "Most insurance policies do not cover house damage done by the insured's own children, which includes foster children. I'm sorry, but even if you could personally guarantee our payment, we can't start today. We've already sent that crew on another job."

"I see." With a feeling of defeat, I hung up the phone and explained the problem to Earl.

"But I told the adjuster Thursday that technically Casey was not under our care," Earl said, puzzled. "Hasn't he checked that yet with the agency?"

We called the adjuster. No, he hadn't had time. It had been a holiday weekend. In addition, they were shorthanded.

I drew in a deep breath and once again smelled the nauseating odors which permeated the house. "But you did find time to cancel the cleaners," I told him. My voice rose. "Don't you understand? This house reeks after setting four days with all this garbage inside. It takes two minutes to make that phone call." My voice started to quiver. I could no longer hold back the tears or my anger.

Earl took the phone from my hand. He, too, felt defeated after he finally hung up. If I had to name a moment that looked very bleak, it was this one.

What if the insurance wouldn't cover the damage? How could we afford to replace what had been destroyed? Who would help us clean? A house of which we were once so proud now stood in mocking ugliness.

"O ye of little faith" (Luke 12:28). How quickly the Lord provided reassurance and answers!

"What is all that commotion?" Earl jumped up after hearing loud voices and a number of car doors slamming outside.

"Would you look at this," he said, staring out egg-stained windows. "I don't believe it!"

"What is it?" I asked. Before I had a chance to walk across the room to the window, our Young Life Bible study kids infiltrated the house through both the front door and the back. Dressed in work clothes and standing with scrub buckets, brushes and rags in hand, they entered—whistling, laughing, joking, and eager to work.

Barb, the organizer and head leader for the group, held out her arms—bucket, brushes, and all. "Never fear when Miller's here!"

"Oh, Barb!" I said. "You are fantastic!"

"How ya doin', Earl, Pat!" Tim hugged us both.

"Hey, ma, got any Lysol? I left mine home."

"Sorry, Sarah, I'm fresh out."

"Jodi and I want to sort through the pile of books downstairs," one teenager announced.

"I've got dibs on cleaning Pat's jewelry box," someone else piped in.

"Watch it, John!" cried still another. "You're tracking bean soup all over the house."

Their arrival was like a gift straight from heaven. The laughter and joviality of the dozen or so kids was just what Earl and I needed to put the right perspective on our problems. And the kids couldn't wait to dig in. Varying numbers each day throughout spring vacation would make themselves available to help with some really major cleaning jobs.

While I delegated cleaning assignments, Earl answered the phone. A few minutes later, he entered the living room.

"Well," he said after taking a deep breath, "the adjuster just told me our insurance will cover the damages." The crowd cheered.

"Praise the Lord!"

"All right!"

"Fantastic."

Earl continued, "Technically, Casey was in Tom's care and no longer a member of our household."

When Tom assumed parental responsibilities for Casey, I thought God was providing for Casey. Now I understood He actually was providing for

A NEGATIVE TURNS INTO POSITIVES

us.

Slowly—all too slowly, it seemed—I was beginning to realize the importance of Jesus' words to His followers about worry and anxiety as found in Matthew 6:25-34. Verses 33 and 34 spoke directly to me. "But seek ye first the kingdom of God, and his righteousness; and all these things shall be added unto you. Take therefore no thought for the morrow: for the morrow shall take thought for the things of itself. Sufficient unto the day is the evil thereof." In other words, live one day at a time!

Over the next three-month period, we did, indeed, live one day at a time. And the Lord provided. Dinner invitations. Offers to donate furniture and clothing (much of our clothing had been spray painted). An offer by our church to establish a special fund. Lots of cleaning help. And, above all, much, much love, reassurance, and affirmation.

The vandalism was a negative act. But from it were raised many positives. God's name was indeed glorified through a newspaper feature story that focused on the actions of our teenage, Bible-studying cleanup crew. Family relationships were strengthened as we worked together as a team to reestablish a home which had been fourteen years in the making. The rallying of so many friends, relatives, and neighbors to our support was indeed one large blessing comprised of so many individual blessings!

But the Lord didn't stop there. He gave us new

meaning to an old insight. The vandalism indicated just how impermanent material possessions really are. It was so easy to become encumbered by personal belongings and the protection that goes along with ownership. How free Jesus was when He walked our earth because He had no tangible possessions! Unencumbered, He could concentrate on teaching us the intangible purpose, the very essence, of living on earth—to spread the good news of salvation and eternal life through Him.

And, as if that weren't enough, God also threw in a few answers to prayer. Several months earlier, Earl and I had attended a faith seminar conducted by Russ Johnston, author of *God Can Make It Happen*. At the seminar we made prayer lists in which we were encouraged to list not only concerns for others, but also our own wants, needs, and desires. On that list was our desire to pay off our van, assume from my parents the payments on the mobile home at the farm, and an ability to buy new carpeting for the living and dining rooms.

Not only do we have new carpeting throughout the house, but we also have fresh paint and wallpaper for every room. Rather than replace much of what was lost, we used the insurance settlement to pay off our van. The payments ordinarily set aside for the van were then used to assume the mobile home payments.

A NEGATIVE TURNS INTO POSITIVES

God had turned a negative into so many positives! Not only for us, but for Casey too.

Jack Cable learned visiting hours at the juvenile detention center were few and far between—Sunday afternoons for two hours and Wednesday evenings for one.

Later on that same afternoon, Jack stopped by to see us.

"I'm going to visit Casey Wednesday night," he told us. Earl was not yet ready to see Casey. I, too, did not understand his act of destruction against a family who loved him very much. But I still wanted to see him—to talk to him, to let him know we still cared.

"Jack, I'd very much like to see Casey," I said.

"I'll pick you up Wednesday night at seven," he replied.

But by Wednesday night Casey was gone. He had been moved to the county where he once lived with his family. After a hearing, he was placed in a reputable boys' home. There he receives benefits not available in a foster family home—psychological counseling and testing, an individualized education, and security in numbers.

Not all foster children cope well in family environments, one caseworker informed us. Relationships are too close for some who fear making themselves vulnerable to the possibility of further rejection. In a group home they feel safe. They may choose not to form close relationships if they wish.

Casey had built a shell around his innermost feelings after being rejected for so many years. Perhaps that is why he resisted any probing. ("I don't like it when you always ask me a question like what's the matter or something like that. What I am saying is that I want to be alone.")

At the boys' home, Casey can more freely be alone without causing concern. Here he can hide his feelings when he chooses. He is safe in the security of numbers.

> In the day of my trouble I will call upon thee:
> for thou wilt answer me. (Ps. 86:7)

chapter seventeen

And the Lord Makes Lemonade!

There is a lot of truth to the saying, "When life gives you lemons, make lemonade." When some of our foster care experiences looked very negative, the Lord turned them into "lemonade." Letting go of Jenny and Ann was very difficult. I feared they were returning to a little, if any, improved home situation. We would no longer be a part of their lives, and they would lose much of what we had taught. Thank God for proving me wrong!

Casey and Craig's act of vandalism seemed like a real "lemon" at the time. But the "lemonade" God made from that still overwhelms me!

Nine-year-old Jason was a real discipline problem at first. (After Casey left, Jason lived with us for a four-month period before being reunited with his family.) He would almost rather fight with a friend than play with him. One day the school principal called me to come and get Jason. During lunch period he had emptied a salt shaker in a boy's face and poured ketchup on his shirt. Those kinds of days seemed like real "lemons."

Today Jason calls nearly every week, wondering

how we are. He frequently asks about our minister and the Sunday school class he was in. He can't wait for his birthday—a day we promised to come see him. Last week he appeared unannounced at our doorstep while his father waited outside in an old car.

I wouldn't want to retract a single "lemon" day we had during our foster care experiences! Yet I know we can no longer be an effective foster family. The commitment each of us once had has changed. The unity we once felt is gone. Although this may seem negative, I believe this, too, the Lord will work to His glory. I can't help but feel that Mark and Matt's experiences with foster care as children will some day bear fruit upon their maturity.

And, too, the fact that the Lord has blessed my writing so abundantly leads me to believe that perhaps He wants to use me in this way. Published articles based on our experiences seem to be one indication of this. The interest expressed in this book is another. But it continues even further.

Two days ago the editor of a growing women's newspaper in our community spoke of her interest to advertise the need for homes for displaced children. Would I be willing to contact the appropriate agencies to (1) establish a need; (2) research case histories; and (3) prepare copy for publication? Would I! I discovered a great need for this type of publicity. This, too, can be a tool for serving the

AND THE LORD MAKES LEMONADE!

Lord in the field of foster care. Perhaps these "ads" will uncover some committed Christian parents in our community who are willing to be used—used by God for His purposes.

Probably one of the biggest projects of my life has been writing this book. Over the past two years, it has been edited, revised, and rewritten as circumstances and changes occurred. Many people have prayed about it. Much thought, prayer, and research have gone into it.

When telephone interruptions and the hindrances of a daily living routine obstructed the power to concentrate, I packed up a suitcase full of books, research, and writing material to retreat to the quiet solitude of the farm.

Many doubts impeded progress. During these periods of frustration, prayer helped calm the mind. When in my humanness this too failed, somehow God always sent His affirmation in another way. I can't help but recall, for example, a month ago when the organizing and writing seemed to be an overwhelming task entirely too big for me to handle. But, as if a go-ahead sign from the Lord, within a four-day period all four of the children we had fostered called by phone—in the order in which they lived in our home, no less.

First, it was Jenny and Ann. ("Why haven't you answered my letter?" Ann wondered.) Their call was followed by a five-day visit. Since they left us, we and the Millers have been able to assume a supportive role with this family. Periodically, the girls stay with us or we get together for a meal and fun and fellowship. Evidence of their Christian faith adorns their home in the form of plaques and pictures. They now are affiliated with a small Christian church in their community.

A day or two later, Casey called—a real surprise! It has been nearly eighteen months since he left. His only contact with us was by a phone call several weeks after he started living at the boys' home. At that time he reversed the long-distance charges and asked for me. Earl told the operator I wasn't home—that he should call back in a couple of hours. He never returned the call.

This time Casey asked for Mark. I didn't recognize his voice, which had changed to that of a young man's. As I worked, their lengthy conversation, punctuated by laughter, drifted up to my office.

"He said he has settled down, mom, and that he would like to see us again," Mark later told me excitedly. I fully expect him to appear at our doorstep one day as Craig has done. (Though Craig didn't apologize for his part in the vandalism, his contrite manner suggested he was seeking forgiveness.)

And, finally, nine-year-old Jason called to remind me of his upcoming birthday. I shouldn't forget about my promise to come see him on this special day, he reminded me.

AND THE LORD MAKES LEMONADE!

What better affirmation could the Lord send than contact initiated by all four of the children we fostered?

Just as I believe He led us into foster care, so also do I feel His guidance now into a different phase—that of making more people aware of foster care so that others might serve the Lord through foster parenting. But with a word of caution. An inclination to enter the foster parent ranks must be tempered with self-analysis and direction from Him. Just as we are not all gifted to be teachers, ministers to the sick, or peacemakers, so also can we not all be foster parents.

Several years ago, a special issue (Nov.-Dec. 1976) of *Children Today* was devoted to the subject of foster care. In it was a report based on questions raised by a foster parent group from Boise, Idaho, to a panel of former foster children. The article states the results were so electrifying that it prompted the State Department of Health and Welfare to reappraise some licensed foster family homes. The sessions helped make the Casey Family Program (the private foster care agency in Boise with its own foster parent group) aware of the need for initial training for prospective foster parents, in addition to ongoing training throughout the foster care period.

Seven former foster children, who ranged in age from their early twenties to thirty-one, felt, according to the article, that "although a love for children and an ability to demonstrate this love" were the most important prerequisites to foster parenting, "the motives which actually prompt persons to become foster parents were very much suspected. In retrospect, the panelists felt the foster parents with whom they had been placed too often took in children for the money they were paid, for the work the children could perform, or for the status foster parenthood bestowed." (Still, the panelists conceded that their lives probably would have been much worse had it not been for these periods in foster care.)

The panelists also noted they were not told the reasons for their placements and that placements were made on a crisis basis. They often wondered what they had done to cause this moving. "Fear, the panelists felt, was the strongest emotion they had experienced in foster care—fear of what was going to happen, fear of the unknown."

In our experiences, caseworkers seemed to be overloaded with cases. Meetings between foster children and their social workers are too few or under adverse conditions. Lighter caseloads would allow social workers to apply preventive measures to curb unhealthy situations or potential problems by meeting periodically with the foster child and his foster family. Case planning, in which certain goals are set to a fixed time period, can help prevent children from languishing in foster care. Some states have implemented an annual review to determine the child's status on a yearly basis.

There is a great need for foster parents today. The ranks have dwindled. Many women are working to keep up with our present economy. Foster parents are a changing population as people discover they can't handle certain aspects of foster care. But quality means more to foster care than quantity.

Rather than have a large group of untrained foster parents, I would opt to see a small quality group professionally trained and educated to the role of foster parenting. To fill the gap in lost numbers, supervised group homes that house six to eight children may be a viable alternative. One method which reduces the need for foster homes and removes children more quickly from the in-limbo state of foster care is adoption planning with the aid of subsidies. This allows financial aid to families willing to adopt children who would otherwise remain in foster care.

But still another aspect must be considered. While preparation and commitment are necessary prerequisites to becoming an effective foster parent, I believe fostering is much like a marriage or having children of one's own. We prepare and educate ourselves—attend as many homemaking, money management, relationship, and child preparation courses as possible. But we still have no way of knowing what pain and pleasure lies ahead or how to cope with every conceivable problem that might crop up. Knowledge, to be sure, helps us effectively handle many problems. But the real answer lies upon reliance in the Lord Jesus Christ. "He that believeth on me as the scripture hath said, out of his belly shall flow rivers of living water" (John 7:38).

I have always received great comfort in knowing that I am free to fail. No matter what kind of choice I may make—good, bad, or mediocre—as a Christian I know that eventually He will work it out to every believer's overall best interests.

Sometimes it is easy to become overanalytical in trying to reach decisions. We consciously list all the pros and cons of an issue such as foster care, review our list, add and subtract from it—all in an effort to reach a decision that will give the best effects to ourselves and to those we love. This is good. But sometimes the best of efforts fail. Through Christ we know "all things work for good to them that love God" (Rom. 8:28).

In writing this I can't help but think of one couple in our church who at this very time are laboring toward a decision about ten-year-old Shelly. After acting periodically as "weekend" parents for Shelly over the past year, the couple has been approached about taking Shelly as a foster child.

The decision is a difficult one. Shelly is considered an emotionally disturbed child. Some of her behavior is difficult to accept. Bringing an emotionally disturbed ten-year-old child into the lives of a middle-aged couple who have remained childless would be a tremendous adjustment. Yet they love her very deeply as she does them. Their Christian love and influence has been a stabilizing force in Shelly's life.

Knowing their decision will "work for good to them that love God" is a great comfort.

And now we are four. After being a family of five and even six, that too may sound negative. But I can assure you that the Lord continues to make lemonade!

At this very moment He breaks down what once looked like insurmountable obstacles. In another two weeks (after Mark and I return from what is sure to be a fulfilling experience at a Young Life camp nestled in the beauty of the Rocky Mountains) we will move to the farm.

Mark can pursue with renewed vigor his interest in electronics in an almost new vocational school. Matt will complete his elementary education in a very fine small-town parochial school. Both boys will have front-door bus service.

Wintry, snow-filled country days mean snowmobiling right out of the barn. No more trailering to an appropriate place. Matt can raise his quail in the loft of an old granary. Mark plans to reintroduce life to the old barn by having a pony and perhaps a few chickens. I look forward to country-fresh air and a peaceful environment very much conducive to writing.

And Earl makes it all possible. He will winterize, repair, build, and maintain—so we can enjoy.

Yet the prospect is not entered without trepidation. As with our foster children, once again "letting go" will be difficult. Letting go of relationships built through church and Young Life—with both adults and kids . . . my Sunday school class . . . jogging three times a week at our local university with a Christian group of people . . . our teenage Bible study group.

But we must "let go"—let God be God so He can continue to work through His treasures that He loaned to us. As my Young Life friend Gretchen Boyd says, "Sometimes God makes lemonade the slow squeeze way."

That old traditional hymn, "Take My Life, and Let It Be Consecrated," says it so well. It beautifully expresses one person's plea to be used for the glory of the Lord—a plea to which I too commit my life.

> Take my life and let it be Consecrated, Lord,
>   to thee;
> Take my hands and let them move At the
>   impulse of Thy love.
>
> Take my feet and let them be Swift and beautiful for thee;

AND THE LORD MAKES LEMONADE!

Take my voice and let me sing Always, only, for my King.

Take my lips and let them be Filled with messages for Thee;
Take my silver and my gold, Not a mite would I withhold.

Take my love, my God, I pour At Thy feet its treasure store;
Take myself and I will be Ever, only, all for Thee.

Because thy lovingkindness is better than life, my lips shall praise thee. Thus will I bless thee while I live: I will lift up my hands in thy name. (Ps. 63:3-4)